# Mary Magdalene

# Mary Magdalene

the disciple whom Jesus loved

Anne-Marie Wegh

MAGDALENA
PUBLISHERS

# Table of contents

# I

## The Healing Hands of God

Mary Magdalene is a woman who speaks to the imagination. Countless myths and legends have tried to fill in the gaps which the Bible leaves open regarding her life and her relation to Jesus. A great many books have been written about her with the wildest speculations. Who was this mysterious woman from whom Jesus reportedly had cast out seven demons, and who subsequently began to play a central part in his life? When his disciples have fled, Mary Magdalene stands with Jesus beneath the cross. In all gospels, she is the first to arrive at the tomb of Jesus, to discover that he is no longer there. In the gospels of John and Mark, she is even the first to whom he appears after his resurrection.

# Universal message

To get to the truth about who Mary Magdalene was, and which part she played in the life of Jesus, we need insight in the Bible's symbolism. And an open mind. The Bible writers did not independently invent the godly wheel. In both the Old and the New Testament, we can find influences of other traditions which were concerned with the greater realities. Those who are open to this will have little trouble identifying aspects of eastern traditions (for instance the chakra teachings) and the divine myths of, among others, ancient Egypt and the ancient Greeks.

The Creator of our universe has communicated with his creatures throughout the history of mankind. All that has been put to paper about this, and still today is studied by believers and scientists, is colored by the frame of reference of the receiver: by his or her culture, received wisdom, and the perspectives of the times. The words and images may therefore differ per prophet, but whoever can see through the exterior, the rituals and rules, clearly sees the red thread that connects all spiritual traditions.

### *Process of spiritual growth*

Our reality is defined by duality. Our senses observe the world in contrasts: dark-light, life-death, man-woman, and so on (Taoism speaks of yin and yang). The divine dimension, on the other hand, is signified by oneness.

The duality of matter is also reflected in our inner world. At the energetic and psychological level, every human being has a feminine and a masculine side.

The central message of virtually all holy texts, whether explicit or hidden in symbolism, is that during our life on earth, we can reconnect to our Creator when we transform our inner duality to a state of unity. This requires an intensive process of purification, during which the ego has to leave the stage.

## Divine energy source in our pelvis

A person cannot accomplish this spiritual growth by their own strength, although some, particularly in the modern self-help spirituality, would love to believe this. To attain this we need an energy source of divine origin, located in our pelvis, near the sacrum. This power source is known by many names. It is the *kundalini-shakti* to the Hindus, the *Shekhinah* of the Jews, and the Holy Spirit of the Christians. The Gnostics called her Sophia (Wisdom). The Biblical book of Job speaks poetically of "the healing Hands of God" (Job 5:18).

When this energy awakens from her inactive, "sleeping" state, she initiates a process of healing and purification within the person. The subconscious is cleaned up: stagnant emotions are processed, surplus psychological ballast is removed, spiritual wounds are healed. This allows the vital energy to flow unobstructed, as in an undamaged child. This state of wholeness is needed for the final objective of the spiritual process: the unification with God.

## The Bible

Our potential to God-realization forms the nucleus of all the divine mythologies in the world. All those adventures of gods, goddesses and mythical animals want to tell us something about our possibility to an inner transformation. If you are able to unravel the symbolism, these stories that at first glance seem hard to believe and sometimes rather primitive, appear to contain great wisdom and beauty.

Also the Bible is full of stories which should be read as metaphors for a process of spiritual growth, to which all people are called. The story of Adam and Eve, who are driven out of Paradise, is about the origin of man's inner dualism. The name Adam is the Hebrew word for human. The Book of Genesis tells that God made Eve out of one of Adam's ribs. The deeper meaning of this is that man is internally divided into a male and a female side.

Many of the marriages that are told of in the Old Testament depict the restoration of the inner unity.


# Divine myths

I would now like to take the reader on a brief tour through the divine myths of Hinduism, Buddhism, ancient Egypt and the ancient Greeks, so that with this knowledge we can clarify the symbolism of the texts in the gospels in which Mary Magdalene is mentioned, and make some surprising discoveries!

In divine families the mother goddess often personifies man's internal divine power source, which most traditions regard as feminine. Other gods and goddesses of the pantheon commonly depict specific aspects of the transformation process.

### Hinduism

The principle of spiritual awakening is based on the premise that with our incarnation on earth, also the divine within a person is split up into two poles, which yearn to reunite with each other.

In Hinduism these poles are depicted as the goddess Shakti (the kundalini), situated in the pelvis, and the god Shiva, residing in the crown chakra. During a spiritual awakening, the kundalini-Shakti rises through the spinal column to the crown, to Shiva. At the level of our forehead the divine couple is reunited. The Hindus call the state of enlightenment that follows the completion of this process *samadhi*.

In chapter 3 we will see that the principle of the inner reunion of the divine couple can also be found in the Bible:
- the encounter of king Solomon with the queen of Sheba;
- in the Song of Songs;
- the marriage between Esther and king Ahasuerus;
- the encounter between Mary Magdalene and the resurrected Jesus at the tomb.

*The goddess Kali*

One of the manifestations of Shakti is Kali. This goddess, with her terrifying appearance, depicts the purifying power of the kundalini-energy. Kali destroys anything that stands between man and God. Traditionally she is depicted wearing a necklace of bloody, severed heads: trophies of all the egos she has destroyed. She sticks het tongue out, which refers to another image that is often used for the kundalini-energy: the serpent. A serpent uses its tongue to catch scents. In the same way, Kali scans the inner self for impurities.

Despite her terrifying image, bloody attributes and impetuousness, Kali is popular among Hindus because her intentions stem from motherly love. She releases her children from their attachments to the ego and the body, and destroys "Maya," the "veil of illusion."

**A Biblical parallel of the inner kundalini-purification process** is the exorcism of Mary Magdalene's demons (chapter 2).

**Decapitation as metaphor for the "death" of the ego** appears in the story of the beheading of John the Baptist (chapter 4).

*The goddess Durga*

In her milder form, Kali is Durga, the warrior goddess with the serene exterior. Also the battle-eager Durga handles her sword for our benefit. She rides a lion. This symbolizes her power over the realm of emotions and animalistic, instinctive drives.

A central theme in all writings on the kundalini mystery is the need to conquer our animal nature. This is an aspect that is connected to the body, which we receive upon our incarnation on earth.

The term "to conquer" is deliberate and carefully chosen. The tendency to want to suppress or deny our animal nature is tempting but it has the opposite effect on the spiritual process. The task is to attain mastery. When our primitive animal drives have been purified and sublimated (transformed), they will help us to realize the divine.

The god Shiva also rides an animal: the white bull Nandi. This is to tell us that the animal nature of Shiva has been purified (white).

**A Biblical parallel of mastery over the animal drives** is the image of Jesus who enters Jerusalem (i.e. a person's heart) riding a donkey (chapter 5).

## Buddhism

Certain schools of Buddhism venerate gods and goddesses. The most important goddess of Tantric Buddhism is Vajrayogini; the feminine counterpart of the Buddha. She embodies the state of enlightenment and rebirth.

*Vajrayogini*

In iconography, Vajrayogini is commonly naked and colored red, surrounded by flames that symbolize the kundalini-fire (*tummo*). Her attributes include a knife with which she severs all attachments, and a skull cup, from which she drinks the elixer of bliss.

When the awakened kundalini has arrived at the brain, the pineal gland, hypothalamus and pituitary gland are stimulated to secrete hormones and opioids into the brain fluid, which results in an experience of the divine and a general vitalization of the body. Tantric Buddhism's elixer of bliss (*mahasukha*) is a metaphor for this sublimated (transformed) brain fluid. Hinduism calls it *amrita* (nectar of immortality).

The illustration shows Vajrayogini positioned on a hexagram. This six-pointed star is a universal symbol of the fusion of the duality (depicted by the two triangles that the hexagram comprises) into divine oneness.

**Biblical references to a change in the brain during the process of spiritual awakening are found with:**
- the resurrection of Lazarus;
- the anointment of Jesus by Mary Magdalene (both in chapter 3).

**The symbol of the hexagram is incorporated by the author of the fourth gospel in:**
- the crucifixion of Jesus;
- the burial of Jesus (both in chapter 4).

*The god Asclepius*

### The Ancient Greeks

The Greek myths are also pervaded by kundalini symbolism. The symbol for medicine and health care, the Rod of Asclepius, is derived from the staff with a serpent of the demi-god Asclepius, who was associated with healing. The serpent, with its ability to renew itself by means of shedding its skin, can be found in virtually all traditions as symbol of the kundalini-energy. Healing is an important aspect of a kundalini process.

*The Rod of Asclepius*

Another staff, the caduceus of the god Hermes, also symbolizes a kundalini-awakening. The staff of the caduceus represents a person's spinal column, through which the kundalini flows upward, with at its top the pineal gland in the shape of a small bulb.

The two serpents that spiral around the staff represent the two energy channels that are involved in a spiritual awakening. Left of the spinal column flows the feminine energy, to the right the masculine. These two energy channels merge at the level of the forehead, in the final phase of the kundalini process.

The wings, atop the staff, symbolize the expanded consciousness of the person who completes the process.

Hermes with caduceus

**In the fourth gospel we find symbology that refers to the caduceus:**
at the baptism of Jesus, at his crucifixion and at his burial (chapter 4).

Of the many Greek gods which represent aspects of the kundalini-process, I will highlight two for our tour: mother-goddess Hera and her messenger Iris. Hera personifies the kundalini-energy in a person's pelvis. She is considered the goddess of marriage and birth: two events which also take place within a person, at the spiritual level, during a kundalini awakening. After the inner merger of the masculine and feminine aspects, also known as the "sacred marriage", the person is "born again" (see chapter 4).

One of Hera's attributes is a staff with either a lotus on top (the spinal column with the opened crown chakra), or an ornament that refers to the pineal gland. According to the myths, Hera's milk would render immortality: referring to the sublimation of the brain fluid during a kundalini awakening.

Mother goddess Hera

The goddess Iris offers a libation

Hera's personal messenger is Iris, the goddess of the rainbow (the chakra colors). Iris has golden wings. She connects the world of the gods and the world of humanity. Among her attributes is the caduceus. These are all aspects that refer to the kundalini-energy.

On the illustration we see Iris offering a libation: she pours liquid onto an animal. With these images an important task of the kundalini-energy is expressed, namely the sublimation (transformation) of the animal (particularly the sexual) drives.

> In the Bible we find the principle of the "preservation" and transformation of the
> sexual energy:
> - in the story of Jacob and the angel;
> - in the story of the fall of Jericho;
> - in the story of Susanna and the two elders;
> - in the story of David and Bathsheba (all in chapter 5).

## Ancient Egypt

One of the most important goddesses of the Egyptian pantheon is Isis, the goddess of marriage, wisdom and health. These are three kundalini aspects (Gnostics call the kundalini Sophia: Greek for Wisdom!). The husband of Isis, Osiris, is also her brother. This peculiarity we also see with the Greek gods. Hera, for instance, is not only the wife of Zeus but also his sister. This incestuous brother-sister relationship is a reference to the division of the singular God into two divine poles (in brother and sister) within a person. Their marriage depicts the unification of the two poles in the aspirant who completes the spiritual transformation process.

> **A Biblical parallel of a marriage between brother and sister** is the marriage of
> patriarch Abraham with his half-sister Sarah (chapter 3).

The best known Egyptian myth is the resurrection of Osiris. In this myth, Osiris is the king of Egypt. He is killed and cut into pieces by his jealous brother Seth. Wife Isis gathers the pieces of his body and joins them again. Only his penis she cannot recover. Via magic she nevertheless manages to conceive of a child with him: their son Horus. Horus succeeds his father as king of Egypt.

This story is about the dying of the old man and the resurrection/birth of the new man as a result of a kundalini awakening. It shows that the old man first has to be completely dismantled during the spiritual process (to be cut into pieces), after which the kundalini-energy (Isis) initiates a process of healing.

Osiris and Isis together (the sacred marriage) beget Horus (the new man) without the use of a penis. The meaning of this is that the birth of the new man (Horus) can only take place when the sexual energies are no longer used by the genitals. With the succession by Horus, the transformation symbology is complete.



Also the Egyptian gods possess various attributes that provide clues about which aspect of the spiritual process of awakening they represent. Particularly the large variation of crowns stand out here. These head coverings refer in many cases to the changes in the brain under the influence of the kundalini.

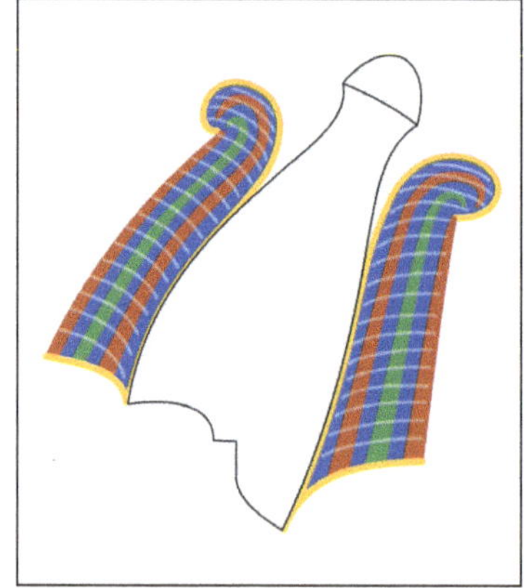

*The god Osiris with Atef-crown*

Osiris often wears the so-called Atef-crown: a white mitre with a bulb (the pineal gland) on top and feathers on the sides. Like the wings of the caduceus, these feathers symbolize the completion of a kundalini process.

On the illustration we see a so-called *Uraeus* cobra (the Egyptian symbol of the kundalini energy) at the level of the forehead of Osiris (the place where the pineal gland is situated). The body of the serpent ascends to the bulb on top of the crown. This refers to the activation of the pineal gland by the "kundalini cobra".

The crook (*heka*) in the hand of Osiris represents the spinal column with the activated kundalini energy. The flail (*nekhakha*) in his other hand refers to the suffering that accompanies a kundalini awakening. The dismantling of the ego (the old person) and is rarely painless. The three ribbons attached to the flail represent the three energy channels which are involved with a kundalini awakening.

**In the gospels,** the suffering that accompanies the letting go of one's old self is depicted by Jesus' way of the cross, and his being scourged per order of Pilate (John 19:1).

## Translation to internal reality

All these myths came into existence to make our inner world visible, and understandable. Within us exists a force field, an arena, in which higher/divine and lower/animal forces compete for dominance. The gods and goddesses, with their specific qualities, represent certain energies. Their life stories represent processes which take place in us, and depict our potential of spiritual growth. The value of these stories is that they are translated to one's personal inner reality. They are invitations to go on the adventures that the divine myths describe.

The same is true for the stories of the Bible. Mary Magdalene and Jesus walked the earth in physical reality. But what has been written about them in the gospels does not constitute a historical report, but rather a bouquet of literary constructions that aim to tell us something about the path to God-realization. These stories too are meant to be translated to one's own inner reality.

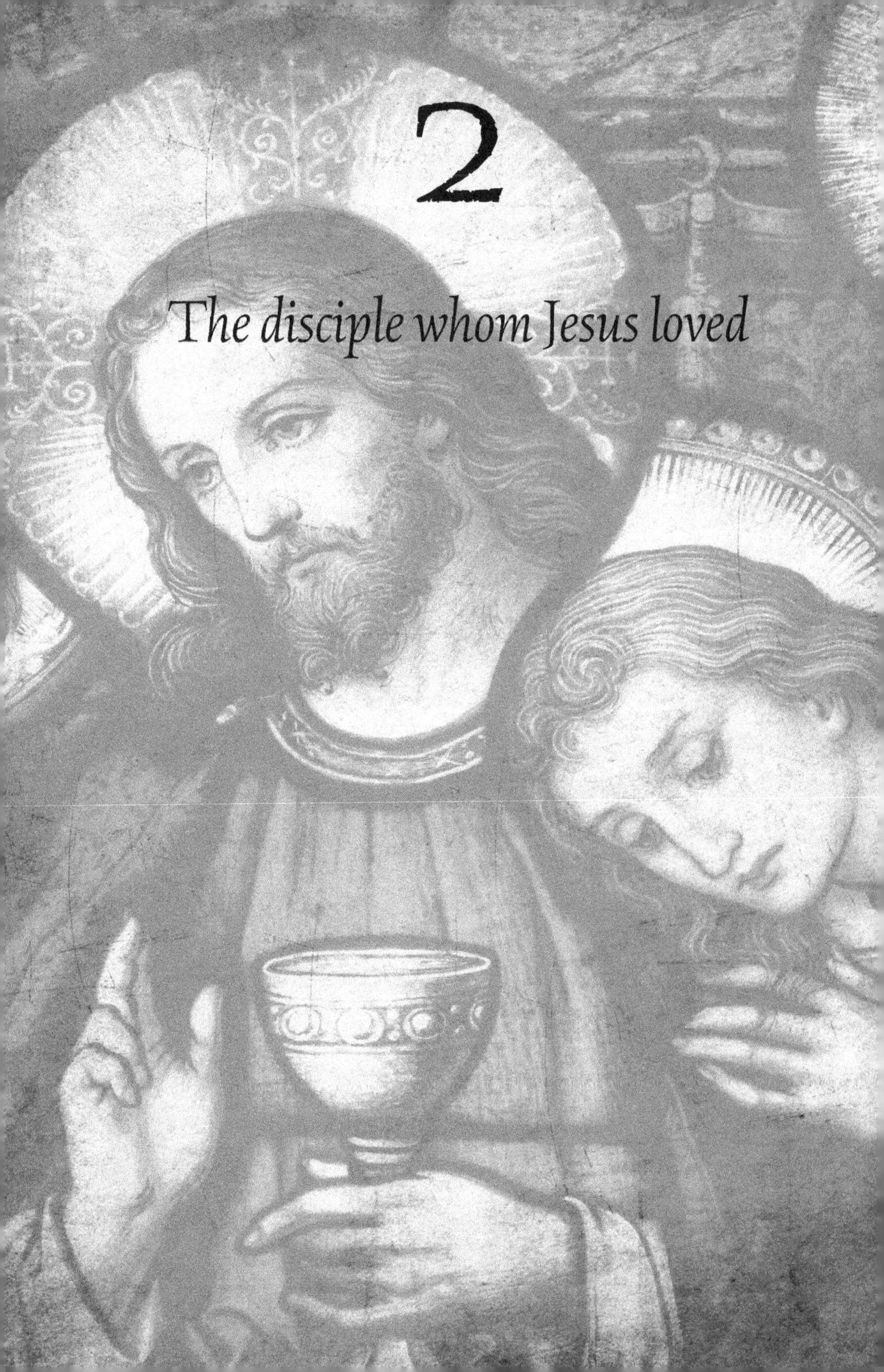

# 2

## The disciple whom Jesus loved

*On that day a fountain will be opened to the house of David and
the inhabitants of Jerusalem, to cleanse them from sin and impurity.*

Zechariah 13:1

The Bible contains very little direct information about Mary Magdalene. She was one of the women who followed Jesus on his tour through Judea, and she was delivered of seven demons. At closer inspection, however, there appears to be a treasure trove of indirect information hidden within the passages in which Mary is mentioned.

This chapter will answer the following questions: Was Mary Magdalene a converted prostitute? Had she been possessed by no fewer than seven demons? When we have removed the labels that have become attached to her, we will aim our searchlight onto the gospel of John, and make an exciting discovery.

## Sinner?

The prostitute image of Mary Magdalene has emerged as a consequence of two passages in the Bible. First, many equate her with the unnamed "sinner" who anoints Jesus' feet in the house of Simon the Pharisee (Luke 7:36-50). The reason why people assume that the sins of this woman relate to prostitution is that, afterwards, Jesus says about her:

> *For this reason I say to you, her sins, which are many, have been forgiven, for she loved much; but he who is forgiven little, loves little.*
> (Luke 7:47)

Some regard a woman "who has loved much" as euphemism for a woman of easy virtue. This reasoning is illogical, as it would mean that the woman is forgiven because she has led a lewd life. It's more probably that Jesus meant it the way it was written: who has loved much, is forgiven much. In any case, the Bible does not state that this sinner is Mary Magdalene.

Directly after the story of the sinner follows a passage that does mention Mary Magdalene:

> *After this, Jesus traveled about from one town and village to another, proclaiming the good news of the kingdom of God. The Twelve were with him, and also some women who had been cured of evil spirits and diseases:* **Mary (called Magdalene) from whom seven demons had come out;** *Joanna the wife of Cuza, the*

*manager of Herod's household; Susanna; and many others. These women were helping to support them out of their own means.*
(Luke 8:1-3)

Also the evangelist Mark makes mention of seven demons with Mary Magdalene, and ascribes their exorcism to Jesus:

*When Jesus rose early on the first day of the week, he appeared first to Mary Magdalene, out of whom he had driven seven demons.*
(Mark 16:9)

She had been possessed, says the Bible, and she was apparently unmarried, or else she would have been called "the wife of…", as was customary in that time. An unmarried woman who followed Jesus - that too didn't favor her image, and has strengthened the suspicion that she indeed was the sinner who had anointed Jesus' feet.

## Demons

For centuries the texts of the Bible were interpreted literally. Christianity reckoned Mary Magdalene a saint, but predominantly because she converted from a life of sin. She became an inspiring example to all who had drifted away from God due to an improper lifestyle, and were contrite. Whoever threw himself at Jesus' feet would be forgiven, just like Mary Magdalene.

Fortunately, an increasing number of people realize that the stories of the Bible should not always be taken literally. The Old and New Testaments are full of symbolism and metaphors that want to convey esoteric wisdom to the spiritual seeker who is ready to receive it ("He who has ears to hear, let him hear…").

Demons represent ego-aspects, which stand between us and God, and an exorcism of seven demons is a metaphor for a spiritual purification process. The number seven refers to Mary Magdalene's chakras, which were purified. She was not possessed but had completed a process of God-realization. She was an "awakened" one.

## Seven chakras

The story of the healing of Mary has parallels in the Bible, with similar meanings. In the Old Testament, for instance, we read about army commander Naaman who suffers from leprosy: a disease that symbolizes spiritual impurity. The prophet Elisha advises him to wash himself seven times in the Jordan:

> *So he went down and dipped himself in the Jordan seven times, as the man of God had told him, and his flesh was restored and became clean like that of a young boy.*
> (2 Kings 5:14)

The seven chakras of Naaman were entirely cleansed, by the Holy Spirit/kundalini (the water of the Jordan), from everything that stood between him and God. He returned to the state of wholeness "of a young boy." This wholeness is required to gain access to the Kingdom of God:

> *I tell you the truth, anyone who will not receive the kingdom of God like a little child will never enter it.*
> (Luke 18:17)

The advice of Elisha to Naaman we may apply to ourselves: someone who sincerely seeks God will have to endure a process of spiritual purification. The name Naaman means pleasantness or loveliness. The purification will make us "pleasant" to God.

In the Book of Revelation we read of a prophetic vision of a scroll of which the seven seals are opened one by one (Revelation 5-8). This scroll is a metaphor for the spinal column. The seven seals represent the seven chakras, which are positioned along the spine and are activated (opened) during the process of spiritual awakening. With the opening of the seventh seal also the doors to the divine open:

> *Then God's temple in heaven was opened, and within his temple was seen the ark of his covenant.*
> (Revelation 11:19)

## *Awakening from duality*

In the gospels, Jesus expels many evil spirits and demons. In the gospel of Matthew we read of a boy who is "moonstruck" (i.e. lunatic, which literally means moonstruck) due to the presence of a demon:

> *14 And when they had come to the multitude, there came to Him a certain man, kneeling down to Him and saying,*
> *15 "Lord, have mercy on my son, for he is lunatic and sorely vexed; for ofttimes he falleth into the fire and oft into the water.*
> *16 And I brought him to Thy disciples, and they could not cure him."*
> *[17] Then Jesus answered and said, "O faithless and perverse generation, how long shall I be with you? How long shall I suffer you? Bring him hither to Me."*
> *18 And Jesus rebuked the devil, and he departed out of him, and the child was cured from that very hour.*
> (Matthew 17:14-18 KJ21)

Lunacy is an archaic word for epilepsy, an affliction which used to be associated with possession. The Greek verb seléniazomai literally means "to be struck by the moon." In that time, epileptic fits were thought to be provoked by the lunar phase.

The always waxing and waning moon is a universal symbol of the non-permanent character of physical reality. Everything on earth is subject to cycles of birth and death, decay and renewal. The moon also symbolizes duality: the opposites from which the earthly reality is constructed. The always shining sun represents the divine, which is eternal, one, and unchanging.

Being influenced by the moon refers to spiritual unconsciousness, to a person who is continuously tossed about by emotions that are provoked by a life in duality, symbolized in this story by falling into water and into fire (verse 15).

The awakened person, who is rooted in the divine, has disconnected him- or herself from his or her emotions. The illusion of duality is exposed and perceived from an unshakeable self. To achieve this imperturbability, many spiritual traditions advise their aspirants equanimity: a way of life that requires no more effort, but is experienced as a natural state of being, at the end of the journey.

The healing of the lunatic boy may be read as an initiation story. Jesus helps him to awaken from duality.

In the Book of Revelation, the human soul is portrayed by a woman "clothed with the sun, with the moon under her feet." Standing on the moon symbolizes victory over duality:

*A great and wondrous sign appeared in heaven: a woman clothed with the sun, with the moon under her feet and a crown of twelve stars on her head.*
(Revelation 12:1)

# Magdalene

That the exorcism of Mary's demons represents a process of God-realization, is confirmed by the epithet Magdalene (meaning "of Magdala"), which was added to her name.

The Greek name Magdala is a transliteration of the Hebrew name Migdal El, which means Tower of God. On several occasions in the Bible, the tower is deployed to serve as metaphor for the spinal column in which the awakened Holy Spirit (kundalini) flows. An inner tower, therefore, which reaches the gates of the Kingdom of God, in the crown chakra.

## *The Tower of Babel*

In the Old Testament we read about the Tower of Babel; a tower that was said to reach into the heavens (Gen 11:1-9). The building of this tower was an audacious act, which God himself put a stop to. It is a story about human pride, with the moral that the Holy Spirit will not allow herself to be utilized as vehicle for the ego. The divine energy in our pelvis awakens when God wills it; not when man wills it.[1]

This is the reason why the knowledge of this power source in our pelvis is hidden from the broader audience, and perhaps could be called the greatest secret of mankind. This knowledge was only shared with spiritual aspirants who were ready for it - who were mature and purified enough to handle it properly. Jesus too warns against trying to obtain the divine single-handedly:

> *And from the days of John the Baptist until now the kingdom of heaven has been treated violently, and violent men take it by force.*
> (Matthew 11:12 NAS)

## Baptism in the Holy Spirit

From the few words regarding Mary Magdalene that the Bible contains, we may deduct that she was found worthy by Jesus to be initiated in the secrets of the Kingdom of God. By him she is "baptized with the fire of the Holy Spirit":

> *I baptize you with water for repentance. But after me will come one who is more powerful than I, whose sandals I am not fit to carry. He will baptize you with the Holy Spirit and with fire. His winnowing fork is in his hand, and he will clear his threshing floor, gathering his wheat into the barn and burning up the chaff with unquenchable fire.*
> (Words of John the Baptist; Matt 3:11-12)

A winnowing fork was used to separate the chaff from the wheat. It was a wooden fork with which the threshed grain was tossed into the air. The heavier grain fell back to the ground and the chaff was carried off by the wind. In the parable, the winnowing fork represents the spinal column, with the purifying, unquenchable fire of the Holy Spirit.

This baptism Mary received from Jesus. With the winnowing fork in his hand (with the fire of the Holy Spirit in his own spinal column) Jesus cleared the threshing floor (chakras) of Mary of chaff (demons, i.e. impurities).

From the honorary sobriquet Magdalene - Tower of God - we can deduct that her spiritual level was considered extraordinary and commanded great respect.

## Building a tower

The spiritual meaning of "Tower of God" is confirmed by Jesus in the gospels. On several occasions he uses the image of a tower when he wants to explain something to his followers about the Kingdom of God. In Luke he warns the multitude that accompanies him that following him has consequences. As with building a tower, he says, it is wise to consider up front whether you are capable of doing it:

> *And anyone who does not carry his cross and follow me cannot be my disciple. Suppose one of you* **wants to build a tower**. *Will he not first sit down and estimate the cost to see if he has enough money to complete it? For if he lays the foundation and is not able to finish it, everyone who sees it will ridicule him, saying, 'This fellow began to build and was not able to finish.'*
> Luke 14:27-30

It would be a curious example if there wouldn't be a deeper meaning behind this, because how many people would, at some point in their lives, consider to build a tower? In this regard, Jesus would better have referred to the building of a house, to clarify his point. But Jesus chooses his examples carefully. Following him means to commence the spiritual process that he completed successfully: a long, arduous journey of intensive purification ("carrying your cross"), and rebuilding your spinal column into a "tower that reaches into the heavens."

### A tower in a vineyard

In another parable, Jesus compares the Kingdom of God with a vineyard containing a tower. This vineyard the landlord (i.e. God) rents out to the workers (man):

> *Hear another parable: There was a certain householder who planted a vineyard, and hedged it round about, and dug a wine press in it, and* **built a tower**, *and let it out to husbandmen and went into a far country. And when the time of the fruit drew near, he sent his servants to the husbandmen, that they might receive the fruits of it. And the husbandmen took his servants, and beat one and killed another and stoned another.*
> (Matthew 21:33-35 KJ21; also see Mark 12:1-3)

The moral of this parable is that God has given man a great spiritual growth potential (the vineyard). In the Bible, wine represents the divine. Most people, however, do nothing with their divine potential (they don't produce fruits). Prophets (the servants in the parable), who proclaim the message of God and try to convert people, are beaten, stoned or killed. Jesus warns them: Therefore I tell you that the kingdom of God will be taken away from you and given to a people who will produce its fruit. (Matt 21:43)

Also in this parable, Jesus chooses his words carefully. The mere image of the rented vineyard would have sufficed. By also mentioning a tower, those 'who have ears' know enough: this is about the inner realization of the Kingdom of God.

## Conclusion

Nowhere in the Bible is written that Mary Magdalene was a prostitute. But what is written, appears to refer to a high spiritual status:

> … *Mary (called Magdalene) from whom seven demons had come out, …*
> (Luke 8:2)

What the evangelist Luke wants to tell us with this is: *Maria was called the Tower of God **because** seven demons had come out from her.*
Her seven chakras had been purified and through her spinal column flowed the fire of God's Spirit.

## Special connection

Mary Magdalene occupied a special place among the disciples of Jesus. Not only her title of honor points this way, but also her presence during all important events surrounding Jesus' crucifixion and resurrection. When we add to her spiritual level the fact that, according to the gospels, Jesus' other disciples often did not understand him, it becomes not difficult to imagine that Jesus and Mary were closely connected.

She herself uses the term "to love" when she describes this connection in the account that she has left us, regarding everything she has learned from Jesus. This account has been incorporated into the New Testament, under the name the Gospel of John…!

# The disciple whom Jesus loved

The identity of the author of the fourth gospel has been topic of research and debate for nearly two thousand years. According to received wisdom, it is the apostle John, but in modern times many experts doubt this.

Judging from the content of the gospel, it must have been someone who was very close to Jesus. The anonymous author says to report from first hand, about what he has seen with his own eyes, and calls himself the "disciple whom Jesus loved":

> *20 Peter turned and saw that the disciple whom Jesus loved was following them. (This was the one who had leaned back against Jesus at the supper and had said, "Lord, who is going to betray you?")*
> *24 This is the disciple who testifies to these things and who wrote them down. We know that his testimony is true.*
> (John 21:20, 24)

Why would the author have chosen for anonymity? Several reasons can be thought of, but a very good reason would be because it was a woman!

Women were commonly not taken serious in those days, which is also made clear in a galling passage in the gospel of Luke. When Jesus, after his death, has appeared to a number of women, and they rush to tell of this to the male apostles, they are not believed:

> *When they came back from the tomb, they told all these things to the Eleven and to all the others. It was Mary Magdalene, Joanna, Mary the mother of James, and the others with them who told this to the apostles.*
> *But they did not believe the women, because their words seemed to them like nonsense.*
> (Luke 24:9-11)

Full as she was about what she had learned from Jesus, Mary decided to write her own version of the "good message"[2]. She chose to remain anonymous and assume a male profile in her texts. She deliberately made the audience suspect that this man was the apostle John, as we shall see shortly.

## The disciple whom Jesus loved (quotes)

### The exposure of Judas

*When Jesus had thus said, He was troubled in spirit, and testified and said, "Verily, verily I say unto you that one of you shall betray Me." Then the disciples looked at one another, not knowing of whom He spoke. Now there was leaning on Jesus' bosom* **one of His disciples, whom Jesus loved**. *Simon Peter therefore beckoned to him, that he should ask who it should be of whom He spoke. He then, leaning on Jesus' breast, said unto Him, "Lord, who is it?"*
(John 13:21-25 KJ21)

### The crucifixion

*Near the cross of Jesus stood his mother, his mother's sister, Mary the wife of Clopas, and Mary Magdalene.*
*When Jesus saw his mother there, and* **the disciple whom he loved** *standing nearby, he said to his mother, "Dear woman, here is your son,"*
*and to the disciple, "Here is your mother." From that time on, this disciple took her into his home.*
(John 19:25-27)

### The resurrection

*Now on the first day of the week Mary Magdalene came early to the tomb, while it was still dark, and saw the stone already removed from the tomb.*
*So she ran and came to Simon Peter and to* **the other disciple whom Jesus loved**, *and said to them, "They have taken the Lord from the tomb, and we do not know where they have put Him."*
*So Peter and the other disciple left, and they were going to the tomb.*
(John 20:1-3 NAS)

### The appearance at the Sea of Tiberias

*Early in the morning, Jesus stood on the shore, but the disciples did not realize that it was Jesus.*
*He called out to them, "Friends, haven't you any fish?" "No," they answered.*
*He said, "Throw your net on the right side of the boat and you will find some." When they did, they were unable to haul the net in because of the large number of fish.*
**Then the disciple whom Jesus loved** *said to Peter, "It is the Lord!" As soon as Simon Peter heard him say, "It is the Lord," he wrapped his outer garment around him (for he had taken it off) and jumped into the water.*
(John 21:4-7)

However, in an ingenious way, she left a key in the text, with which the true identity of the author could be retrieved. For this, we have to turn to the Greek source text.

### The hidden key

In the gospel of John, the formula "the disciple whom Jesus loved" appears five times. Four times, the author chose to use the Greek verb *agapaó* (from *agápe*), for the meaning of to love (see opposite page). However, in the passage that describes the discovery of the astonished disciples that the tomb is empty, the Greek verb *phileó* (from *philos*) is used:

> *Now on the first day of the week Mary Magdalene came early to the tomb, while it was still dark, and saw the stone already removed from the tomb.*
> *So she ran and came to Simon Peter and to **the other disciple whom Jesus loved**, and said to them, "They have taken the Lord from the tomb, and we do not know where they have put Him."*
> *So Peter and the other disciple left, and they were going to the tomb.*
> (John 20:1-3 NAS)

In this passage, Mary Magdalene is together with two other disciples present at the empty tomb of Jesus. By calling one of the two men the beloved disciple, making use of another word for to love, her identity as author remains hidden, but she does not deny herself. Through this construction, she can maintain that it was she who first saw the resurrected Jesus.

Also the word "other" stands out in this quote: *the **other** disciple whom Jesus loved*. Together with the other word for to love, and Mary Magdalene's presence in this scene, there is only one logical conclusion: she is the author of this gospel!

A literary construction that is as simple as it is brilliant, and which all this time has successfully hidden that the author of this gospel is a woman. A well-kept secret that allowed her story to be taken seriously and make it through the strict selection process of the early Christian Church fathers, because of which it now is part of the New Testament. This is an honor that did not befall many other gospels from that time. As a consequence her words are read and lavishly cited, across the world and until today.

## The disciple who testifies to these things

Peter turned and saw that **the disciple whom Jesus loved** was following them. (This was the one who had leaned back against Jesus at the supper and had said, "Lord, who is going to betray you?")

When Peter saw him, he asked, "Lord, what about him?"

Jesus answered, "If I want him to remain alive until I return, what is that to you? You must follow me."

Because of this, the rumor spread among the brothers that this disciple would not die. But Jesus did not say that he would not die; he only said, "If I want him to remain alive until I return, what is that to you?"

This is the disciple who testifies to these things and who wrote them down. We know that his testimony is true.

(John 21:20-24)

## Selfless love

When Mary describes the connection she has with Jesus, she uses the word *agápe*, which also says something about the special bond that she has with him.

The ancient Greeks distinguished four kinds of love:

*Agápe*  ➤ charity, neighborly love, selfless love
*Eros*  ➤ physical love, sexuality
*Philos*  ➤ friendship, the love between peers
*Storgē*  ➤ affection, the natural love between parent and child

In Greek eyes agápe is the highest form of love. This love is without sexual attraction (*eros*). Agápe is not based on one's own needs. It is unconditional love.

By using the word *agápe*, Mary in fact provides an answer to that pressing question: did she have an intimate relationship with Jesus; were they lovers? Judging from the choice of words in her gospel, the answer is: no. In chapter 5 we will discuss this issue more elaborately.

### Christian art

Throughout the centuries, there has always been a small group of initiated, artists and mystics who knew that the gospel of John was written by Mary Magdalene. In Christian iconography, the apostle John is commonly depicted as a beardless youth with feminine aspects. In many paintings the evangelist is so obviously a woman that the artists must have meant this as a message for us.
Sometimes John is even so feminine that he is only recognizable by his attributes: a Bible with stylus, an eagle, and/or a drinking cup with or without poisonous serpents. See examples on pages 37 and 38.

Because of the rigid attitude of the church, the truth couldn't be publicly spoken, but covertly she found a way via the painter's canvass. Voices from a distant past speak to us from the walls of museums, churches and cathedrals: Mary Magdalena was the "apostle to the apostles." She was Jesus' most beloved disciple!

Now that we have identified the author of the gospel of John, also some other puzzle pieces fall into place.


## Lazarus

In the fourth gospel, Jesus performs seven "miraculous signs":
1. The wedding at Cana (John 2:1-11)
2. The healing of the official's son (John 4:46-54)
3. The healing at the pool of Bethesda (John 5:1-9)
4. The feeding of the five thousand (John 6:1-14)
5. Jesus walk on water (John 6:16-21)
6. The healing of a man born blind (John 9:1-7)
7. The raising of Lazarus from the dead (John 11:1-44).

People with knowledge of eastern chakra-psychology, who study these remarkable events, will discover that they describe the activation of the seven chakras, along the spinal column, under the influence of the kundalini-energy.[3]

It is not difficult to see a link with the author's own process of awakening: the seven miraculous signs describe the "exorcism of seven demons" which Mary Magdalene herself had experienced.

The seventh miraculous sign is the raising of Lazarus from the dead - an event that raises a number of questions:
- How realistic is it that someone who has been dead for four days, and according to bystanders has started to smell (John 11:39), is brought back to life anyway?
- Why are the other three gospels silent about this remarkable event?
- Why did Jesus wait for two more days before departing for Bethany to raise his good friend Lazarus? (John 11:6)
- Who was this Lazarus, who is unmentioned by any of the other gospels?

These peculiarities become much more logical when we take this story not literal, but as a metaphor for an initiation. Lazarus has not passed away, but is merely "dead" in a spiritual sense. In other words: he is "sleeping" (not yet awakened). Jesus says this explicitly:

## Paintings and stained glass depicting the evangelist John

37

a.

b.

c.

a. *Fyodor Brundi, circa 1840, National Museum, Arkhangelsk, Russia.*
b. *Defendente Ferrari, detail, circa 1525, Philadelphia Museum of Art.*
c. *Domenico Zampieri (Domenichino), 1625-28, Bob Jones University Museum, Greenville, South Carolina.*

d.

e.

f.

g.

d.  Jean Bourdichon, 1503-1508, National Library of France, Paris.
e.  Hans Baldung, 1515, Metropolitan Museum of Art, New York.
f.  Sisto Badalocchio, 1605-1625, location unknown.
g.  John La Farge, 1889, McMullen Museum of Art, Boston, Massachusetts.

*Our friend Lazarus has fallen asleep; but I am going there to wake him up* (John 11:11).

He lies in a cave with a stone against it; symbolizing a person who is locked within his body and matter. Also the strips of linen with which his feet and hands are wrapped represent the lack of freedom of the "sleeping" person (John 11:38,44).

The raising of Lazarus from the "dead" refers to another, in that time widely known, resurrection from the dead: that of the god Osiris from the Egyptian mythology. As we saw in chapter 1, the death and resurrection of Osiris represent the process of spiritual awakening: the old man "dies" and the new man "rises up". The name Osiris in Hebrew is *El Aser* or *El Ausar*. The name Lazarus in Hebrew is *Eleazar*. They are nearly identical.[4]

### Catacombs

In the catacombs of Rome are frescos from the 4th century AD, that depict the raising of Lazarus from the dead. They unmistakably contain kundalini symbolism. On the images (on the next page), we see Jesus who touches the head of Lazarus with a stick, which refers to the activating of the pineal gland.

Two of the images show a pillar, in the top half of the frame. This refers to the Djed-pillar and the ritual of "raising the Djed"; a ritual from ancient Egypt that corresponds with the resurrection of Osiris and which depicts a kundalini-awakening. The pillar symbolizes the spinal column.[5]

From a cloud, someone (God?) throws something (fire?) onto the pillar.

Two of the images show a ladder with seven steps next to the tomb of Lazarus. This ladder too refers to a process of kundalini awakening: the divine energy rises from the pelvis, via the seven chakras, to the crown.

A few clues confirm that the story of Lazarus is about an initiation that Mary Magdalene herself has experienced:
- The author begins to use the qualification "the disciple whom Jesus loved" in chapter 13. Lazarus is no longer mentioned after chapter 12. This could mean that Lazarus is the author of the fourth gospel.

*Frescos from the catacombs of Rome, 4ᵗʰ century AD.*

- The evangelist also says about Lazarus and his two sisters that Jesus loved them, and again uses here the Greek verb *agapaó* (John 11:5).
- The two sisters of Lazarus are called Martha and Maria. The evangelist does not explicitly call Mary "the Magdalene", but she indeed could be Mary Magdalene.
- Not in any of the other gospels we can find any trace of this remarkable miracle. This is curious, also since the story mentions many witnesses.

These elements make it probable that the story of the raising of Lazarus is in fact the final conclusion of what the evangelists Luke and Mark have called an exorcism of seven demons from Mary Magdalene. With the fictitious name Lazarus, which refers to the Osiris myth, Mary informs the reader about the deeper meaning of this "miraculous sign."

This conclusion is seamlessly met by the fact that the author mentions the full name Mary Magdalene only after the resurrection of Lazarus. Before this miraculous sign the text makes mention only of a Mary of Bethany. The resurrection of Lazarus has made Mary a *Migdal El*, a "Tower of God"; an awakened one!

Now that all the puzzle pieces have fallen into place, a final detail stands out. When the synoptic gospels discuss the women who followed Jesus, Mary Magdalena is always mentioned first, which all the more cements her important position among the followers of Jesus. In the fourth gospel, however, she is mentioned last among the women who were present at the cross: *Near the cross of Jesus stood his mother, his mother's sister, Mary the wife of Clopas, and Mary Magdalene* (John 19:25). This is in agreement with proper decorum, even of today: an author always mentions herself last!

### The Last Supper
The supper that Jesus enjoyed with his disciples on the evening before he was crucified is an event that is described in all four gospels. Only in the fourth gospel, the gospel of Mary Magdalene, we read about the disciple who was "leaning on Jesus' bosom".

Leaning on one's bosom, or lap, as the Greek *kolpos* may also be translated, paints a picture of two people who are intimately close. Who understand each other without words. Bosom friends.

Mary was a confidant of Jesus. Or at least in the eyes of the apostles, because when Peter does not understand the words of Jesus, he doesn't ask himself for an explanation but gestures to the author (Mary) to inquire of Jesus what he means:

> *Now there was leaning on Jesus' bosom one of His disciples, whom Jesus loved. Simon Peter therefore beckoned to him, that he should ask who it should be of whom He spoke. He then, leaning on Jesus' breast, said unto Him, "Lord, who is it?"* (John 13:23-25 KJ21)

With the description "leaning on Jesus' bosom," Mary clarifies to us that her heart and the heart of her teacher were connected.

Depictions of the Last Supper are sometimes a source of amusement due to the literal interpretations of "leaning on one's bosom." Not rarely, the confidant of Jesus seems rather comatose. But simultaneously, many paintings contain clear hints to the knowledge of the artists that the privileged position was not occupied by the apostle John but Mary Magdalene. Sometimes John is so feminine that doubt is virtually impossible: the disciple whom Jesus loved was a woman!
(See examples on pages 43 and 44)

## The goddess Io

Let's return briefly to the passage about Mary Magdalene and the exorcism of seven demons, from the gospel of Luke. When we delve deeper into the text, it appears that the author has left a cryptic clue about the spiritual status of Mary Magdalena.

Luke is the only one who mentions Mary Magdalena prior to the crucifixion, and does so in two passages. Both times he mentions, after Mary, a Joanna, who makes no further appearance in any of the other gospels:

a.

b.

c.

a.  Stained glass; location unknown.
b.  Lorenzo Monaco, (detail), circa 1390, Gemäldegalerie, Berlin, Germany.
c.  Mosaic of Semen Zhivago, (detail) 1879-1887, Saint Isaac's Cathedral, St. Petersburg, Russia.

d.

e.

f.

d. *Domenico Ghirlandaio, (detail), 1476.*
e. *Giovanni Antonio Sogliani, (detail), 1511-14*
f. *Gerolamo Romani, (detail) 1533-1534.*

*...and also some women who had been cured of evil spirits and diseases: **Mary (called Magdalene)** from whom seven demons had come out; **Joanna** the wife of Cuza, the manager of Herod's household; Susanna; and many others. These women were helping to support them out of their own means.*
(Luke 8:2-3)

*It was **Mary Magdalene,** Joanna, Mary the mother of James, and the others with them who told this to the apostles.*
(Luke 24:10)

The Greek version of Joanna's name is *Ionna*. Io and Anna are both names of goddesses. Anna is a mother goddess which appears in many traditions.

Like most other mother goddesses, she represents the divine energy in our pelvis (see chapter 1).

### The myth of Io

The eye of supreme god Zeus catches Io, the beautiful priestess of his wife Hera. When Hera finds out, Zeus changes Io into a cow and hides her on earth, behind the cover of clouds. Hera catches on, and instructs the god Argus, a giant with a hundred eyes, to guard the cow so that Zeus cannot reach her. Zeus enlists the god Hermes to free Io. Hera takes revenge by having Io continuously stung by a gadfly, because of which she roams the earth for years in torment. After many wanderings, Zeus returns Io to her human appearance.

Io symbolizes the feminine pole of the one God (the kundalini). She is desired by the masculine pole of the one God (Zeus). Upon an incarnation on earth, she comes to inhabit a human body with animal instincts (the cow), locked in the pelvis (guarded by Argus). The god Hermes (who carries the caduceus, see chapter 1!) liberates Io; the kundalini awakens. The gadfly that stings and torments Io for years symbolizes the kundalini purification process that may cause much discomfort.
Eventually, Zeus gives Io her human appearance back, and she is returned to the world of the gods. This depicts the renouncing of the lower nature (the cow) and the entering of the Kingdom of God, upon the completion of the spiritual process.

*Raffaello Sanzio da Urbino (Raphael), Disputation of the Holy Sacrament, 1510,
Apostolic Palace, Vatican City, Rome*

*While everybody around her busily discusses the institution of the sacred sacrament of the eucharist,
a woman quietly writes. A bishop points toward her.*
*Above, in the clouds, the apostle John is writing too (third character from the left). He looks like a
woman.*
*With images, Raphael shows what in that time could not be spoken: Mary Magdalene is the author
of the fourth gospel.*

*(Also see the painting of Raphael with Mary Magdalene on page 208).*

Io is a Greek goddess. She is a priestess in the court of the goddess Hera. When we closely examine the myth of Io, it becomes clear why Luke forges a link between her and Mary Magdalene. Her story represents a kundalini awakening!

With his double mention of Joanna (*Io-Anna*) after the name Mary Magdalene (the Greek source text has no commas), Luke tells us that Mary is spiritually awakened. Io-Anna is an honorary title, just like Magdalena.

Joanna is *the wife of Cuza*, says the evangelist. The Hebrew word *chusas* means seer. In this context, it is probable that we may regard *"wife of the seer"* as an additional element of the titles of honor of Mary Magdalene: *"Visionary"*.

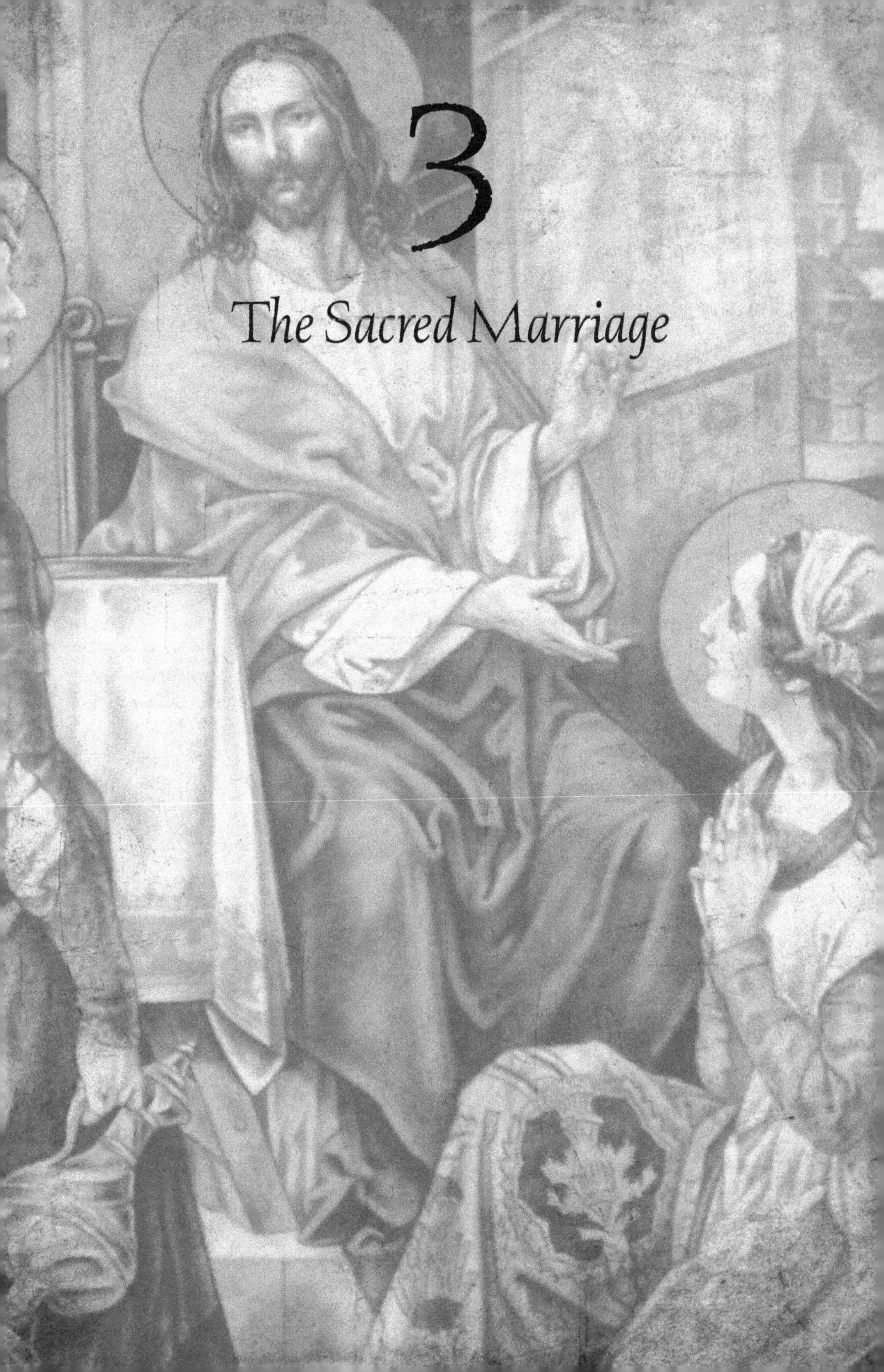
3
The Sacred Marriage

*He who has the bride is the bridegroom…*

John 3:29 (NAS)

In the symbolic jargon of the Bible, our soul is a "widow" because she has lost her connection with God. As long as we are focused on the physical dimensions, she will find no rest. She longs to the sense of fulfilment and bliss that she lost at our birth.

Driven by this longing, we seek our happiness in the outer world; in sensory satisfaction and material things. But whatever we obtain or achieve, nothing can remove the vague restlessness in our hearts.

Internally divided in a feminine and a masculine half, a desire to be whole eats away at us. We embark on an endless quest for the ideal partner that will give us rest and fulfillment. But that which we most deeply desire, and which is so difficult to put into words, we cannot find in another person. For this we must direct our gaze inwardly, where a divine groom awaits us.

This is what the Bible is telling us, using a broad diversity of metaphors. Every story is a gem and can teach us something about the divine.

In this chapter we will first review some examples of Old Testament stories, that are about the merger of the masculine and feminine aspects of a person. This so-called "sacred marriage" results into a unification with God.

After that we will see how in her gospel Mary Magdalene used her own character to demonstrate a kundalini awakening and resulting sacred marriage.

## The symbolic layers of the Bible

In the Old Testament, many marriage partners are found notably at water wells. A well with a shaft, deep into the earth, from which water is brought up, is a fitting metaphor for the kundalini-energy that flows up from the pelvis to the crown, at the moment that the person is ready for the sacred marriage.

Precisely at the right moment, Rebekah brings up drinking water from a well, and so doing becomes the wife of Isaac, the son of patriarch Abraham (Gen 24:15-16).

Jacob, the son of Isaac, meets Rachel at a water well. He removed for her the stone from the well (the kundalini is freed), so that her flocks can drink (Gen 29:9-10). A marriage follows only after seven years (albeit between Jacob and

Rachel's sister Leah). This refers to the seven chakras, which the kundalini must first purify before the sacred marriage can take place.

Moses meets the seven daughters (chakras) of a priest at a well, and proceeds to marry one of them. Her name, Zipporah, means bird. Wings are a classical symbol for the expansion of consciousness, which is the result of an opened seventh chakra (an example of this is the caduceus, the rod of the god Hermes, in chapter 1).

*16 Now a priest of Midian had seven daughters, and they came to draw water and fill the troughs to water their father's flock.*
*17 Some shepherds came along and drove them away, but Moses got up and came to their rescue and watered their flock.*
*18 When the girls returned to Reuel their father, he asked them, "Why have you returned so early today?"*
*19 They answered, "An Egyptian rescued us from the shepherds. He even drew water for us and watered the flock."*
*20 "And where is he?" Reuel asked his daughters. "Why did you leave him? Invite him to have something to eat."*
*21 Moses agreed to stay with the man, who gave his daughter Zipporah to Moses in marriage.*
*22 Zipporah gave birth to a son, and Moses named him Gershom, saying, "I have become a foreigner in a foreign land."*
(Exodus 2:16-22)

The child of Moses and Zipporah (verse 22) represents the reborn "new man." The name Gershom, which means stranger, refers to the feeling of the awakened man of being a "stranger" on earth.

Also the marriage of patriarch Abraham is a depiction of a spiritual process. He is married to his half-sister Sarah: *Besides, she really is my sister, the daughter of my father though not of my mother; and she became my wife* (Gen 20:12).

In the symbolic sense, a marriage within the same family means in the Bible that it is about an *inner* marriage. (See the marriage of Zeus and Hera, and Isis and Osiris, in chapter 1).

Another clue that the bond of Abraham and Sarah is about the sacred marriage is the letter "h," which God adds to their original names Abram and Sarai (Gen 17:5, 15). This Hebrew he, which is also part of YHWH, represents the Spirit of God, or in other words: the kundalini.[6]

## The Queen of Sheba

Perhaps the fairest Biblical metaphor for the sacred marriage is the famous encounter between King Solomon and the Queen of Sheba. It's a brief story but with beautiful and elaborate symbolism. Let's have a look at the details (Bible text on page 54).

The spelling of the name Sheba is as good as identical to the Hebrew word for seven. This mysterious and powerful queen represents the kundalini, which "rules" over the seven chakras.

Jesus calls her "the Queen of the South":

> **The Queen of the South will rise** *at the judgment with this generation and condemn it; for she came from the ends of the earth to listen to Solomon's wisdom, and now one greater than Solomon is here.*
> (Matt 12:42, also see Luke 11:31)

*"The Queen of the South will rise"* is a metaphor for the rising kundalini.

The visit of the queen to Solomon is accompanied by an enormous amount of gifts that are exchanged: symbolic for the inner wealth that a kundalini-awakening brings.

It's said that the reason for the visit is the wisdom of Solomon. In Gnosticism, Sophia is seen as the feminine aspect of God, comparable with the kundalini-shakti of eastern traditions. Sophia is a Greek word, which means wisdom.

The Bible too utilizes a personification of Wisdom to refer to the divine energy in the pelvis. In the Book of Proverbs, for instance, we read about Wisdom:

> *Blessed is the man who listens to me,*
> *watching daily at my doors,*

1   And when the queen of Sheba heard of the fame of Solomon, she came to Jerusalem to test Solomon with hard questions, having a very great company, and camels that bore spices, and gold in abundance, and precious stones. And when she had come to Solomon, she communed with him about all that was in her heart.

2   And Solomon told her all her questions, and there was nothing hid from Solomon which he told her not.

3   And when the queen of Sheba had seen the wisdom of Solomon, and the house that he had built,

4   and the meat of his table, and the sitting of his servants, and the attendance of his ministers and their apparel, his cupbearers also and their apparel, and his ascent by which he went up into the house of the Lord, there was no more spirit in her.

5   And she said to the king, "It was a true report which I heard in mine own land of thine acts and of thy wisdom.

6   However I believed not their words until I came and mine eyes had seen it. And behold, the half of the greatness of thy wisdom was not told me, for thou exceedest the fame that I heard.

7   Happy are thy men and happy are these thy servants, who stand continually before thee and hear thy wisdom.

8   Blessed be the Lord thy God, who delighted in thee to set thee on His throne to be king for the Lord thy God. Because thy God loved Israel, to establish them for ever, therefore He made thee king over them to do judgment and justice."

9   And she gave the king a hundred and twenty talents of gold and spices in great abundance and precious stones; neither was there any such spice as the queen of Sheba gave King Solomon.

10  And the servants also of Hiram and the servants of Solomon, who brought gold from Ophir, brought algum trees and precious stones.

11  And the king made of the algum trees terraces to the house of the Lord and to the king's palace, and harps and psalteries for singers; and there were none such seen before in the land of Judah.

12  And King Solomon gave to the queen of Sheba all her desire, whatsoever she asked, besides that which she had brought unto the king. So she turned and went away to her own land, she and her servants.

(2 Chronicles 9:1-12 KJ21)

*waiting at my doorway.*
*For whoever finds me finds life and receives favor from the Lord*
(Proverbs 8:34-35)

*Wisdom has built her house; she has hewn out its seven pillars.*
(Proverbs 9:1)

And about Jesus we read in the Gospel of Luke that he was filled with wisdom:

*And the child grew and became strong; he was filled with wisdom, and the grace*
*of God was upon him.*
(Luke 2:40)

The feminine aspect of God is called Wisdom, because her awakening in a person leads to gnosis, the knowledge of the heart. The Bible also explicitly says that the wisdom of Solomon was given to him by God in his heart:

*King Solomon was greater in riches and wisdom than all the other kings of the*
*earth. The whole world sought audience with Solomon to hear the wisdom God*
*had put in his heart.*
(1 Kings 10:23-24)

It is wisdom that has been obtained through the personal experience of the divine. The illusion of physical reality (*Maya* in eastern traditions) is exposed. The "veil of the goddess Isis" from the Egyptian myths, which hides the divine from man, is raised.
The Book of Proverbs calls this "*the knowledge of the holy*":

*The fear of the Lord is the beginning of wisdom,*
*and the knowledge of the holy is understanding.*
(Proverbs 9:10 KJ21)

*I [Wisdom] have understanding and power.*
(Proverbs 8:14)

*Sophia (wisdom) from Gnosticism*

*On this illustration, Sophia has a number of attributes which refer to a kundalini awakening. We see a heart that's set ablaze by the divine energy, and is skewered by an arrow (think of the famous mystical experience of the 16th century mystic Teresa of Avila). The sword symbolizes the aspect of inner purification.*

*A large serpent is connected to a globe and crawls along the spine of the skeleton on the ground. The meaning of this is that the divine energy in a person's pelvis also sustains the physical reality (creation, the globe). The globe is positioned under Sophia's feet: the world has been conquered. Above her head hovers a white dove with an olive branch (Noah's dove); symbol of the Holy Spirit. The S-shaped trumpet represents the spiraling movement of the rising kundalini energy.*

*The serpent is wearing a leash, as does the reptile in the right lower corner of the image. This symbolizes the mastery of the lower nature (animal drives); the kundalini energy is no longer used by the lower chakras but is guided upward to the crown (the crown on the head of Sophia).*

The Queen of Sheba gives Solomon *a hundred and twenty talents of gold* (verse 9). We find the deeper meaning of a hundred and twenty when we regard it as the product of twelve times ten. The heart chakra is connected with twelve energy channels.[7] The number ten represents completion, perfection. Gold represents the divine.

The gift of a hundred and twenty talents of gold we may read as: the heart chakra of Solomon is completely purified and opened by the kundalini energy (the Queen of Sheba).

The ascent by which Solomon *went up into the house of the Lord* (verse 4) refers to Solomon's crown chakra, where a connection is made with the transcendental God. Also kundalini-symbolism are the ascending terraces, which the king makes of algum trees (verse 11); a reference to the spinal column. Harps and psalteries - which are made from the same wood - are universal symbols of a kundalini awakening. Strings that are made to vibrate are a metaphor for the activation of the chakras, when within a person, the "queen of the south" sets off on her journey to the crown chakra.

**The pineal gland in art**

In Christian art we find much symbolism that refers to the pineal gland.

The shape of this tiny gland, about the size of a grain of rice, somewhat resembles a pine cone (the French adjective *pinéal* means "like a pine cone"), which explains the name. The pine cone is, like the serpent, a classical symbol of a kundalini awakening.

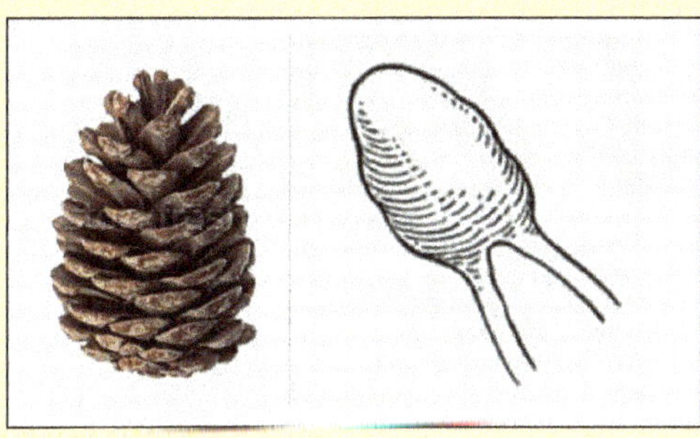

*Piero della Francesca, circa 1452, Meeting between the Queen of Sheba and King Solomon, Basilica of San Francesco, Arezzo, Italy.*

*The robe of Solomon is adorned with a pattern of pine cones. With this, the artist wants to let us know that the meeting between King Solomon and the Queen of Sheba is an internal event, which leads to an activation of the pineal gland.*

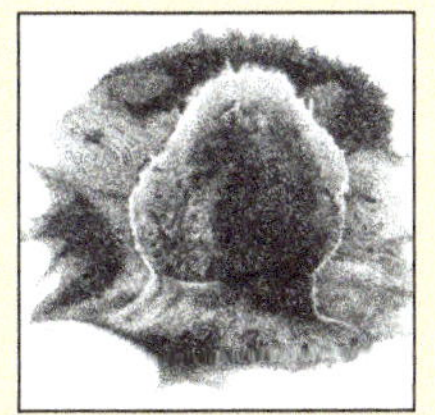

Who develops an eye for it will recognize in Christian art the pine cone, as a symbol, in many ways: as an ornament, for example, and in patterns in wall paper and clothing. (See the examples on pages 58, 60, 77, 198, 204, 210, 217).

*An X-ray image of a pineal gland*

# The Song of Solomon

The Biblical Song of Solomon, or Song of Songs, is a collection of love poems. When we read these texts through the lens of kundalini symbolism, we see unmistakable references to the sacred marriage in the declarations of love. The feminine aspect of God, in a person's pelvis, desires to unite with her masculine counterpole in the crown chakra.

The form of a love poem is in this case not so strange. A kundalini awakening is accompanied by an complete opening of the heart chakra. The awakened person experiences a great love and happiness.

Many metaphors that are used in the Song of Solomon are also used in the rest of the Bible - and outside of the Bible - to describe the kundalini process: fire, lilies, pomegranates, trees, vines, a tower, a fountain, grapes, balm, myrrh, incense, honey, wine, and Paradise.

In the following quotes we will read about:
- a bride who is hidden and enclosed (the kundalini in the pelvis);
- budding and fruit bearing trees and plants (the awakening of the spinal column);
- a groom who incites his beloved to "rise up";
- a groom who descents into the valley (the pelvis) to see if the vine has started to bud;
- lovers who call each other brother and sister. This is a clue that this is an internal process, like with Abraham and Sarah.

*Hans Memling, central panel of the Triptych of St. John the Baptist and St. John the Evangelist, 1479, Hans Memling Museum, Bruges, Belgium*

*On this panel we see the mystical marriage of St. Catherine to the infant Jesus. On the garment of St. Catherine and on the tapestry behind Mary we see references to the pineal gland.*

- In the final quote, the love that is discussed is called "the very flame of the Lord," or in other words: the fire of the kundalini.

*My beloved spoke and said unto me, 'Rise up, my love, my fair one, and come away.*
*For lo, the winter is past, the rain is over and gone.*
*The flowers appear on the earth; the time of the singing of birds is come, and the voice of the turtledove is heard in our land.*
*The fig tree putteth forth her green figs, and the vines with the tender grape give a good smell. Arise, my love, my fair one, and come away.'"*
*"O my dove, that art in the clefts of the rock, in the secret places of the stairs, let me see thy countenance, let me hear thy voice; for sweet is thy voice, and thy countenance is comely."*
(SS 2:10-14 KJ21)

*A garden enclosed is my sister, my spouse, a spring shut up, a fountain sealed.*
*Thy plants are an orchard of pomegranates with pleasant fruits, henna with spike-nard,*
*spikenard and saffron, calamus and cinnamon, with all trees of frankincense, myrrh and aloes, with all the chief spices"*
(SS 4:12-14 KJ21)

*I went down into the garden of nuts to see the fruits of the valley, and to see whether the vine flourished and the pomegranates budded.*
(SS 6:11 KJ21)

*O, that thou wert as my brother, that sucked the breasts of my mother! When I should find thee outside, I would kiss thee; yea, I should not be despised.*
(SS 8:1 KJ21)

*Set me as a seal upon thine heart, as a seal upon thine arm; for love is strong as death; jealousy is cruel as the grave; the coals thereof are coals of fire, which hath a most vehement flame.*
(SS 8:6 KJ21)

We also encounter a warning to not to try to awaken the kundalini on our own initiative, but to wait until it pleases her:

*I adjure you, O daughters of Jerusalem,*
*By the gazelles or by the hinds of the field,*
*That you do not arouse or awaken my love*
*Until she pleases.*
(SS 2:7 NAS)

The bride of the Song of Solomon is dark skinned: *Dark am I, yet lovely...* (SS 1:5). With this she fits the illustrious lineup of black goddesses and Madonnas that appear in many spiritual traditions: the black widow Isis, for example, and Hindu goddess Kali, whose name means "black."

Their dark skin corresponds to the different phases of the kundalini process. The divine energy is associated with three colors:
-   black, when she is still enclosed in the pelvis;
-   red, when she is awakened and her fire purifies the person;
-   white, when the purification process is completed.
A black goddess or Madonna - as well as the bride of the Song of Solomon - depicts the hidden and not yet awakened feminine aspect of God within a person.

## Esther and King Ahasuerus

The Biblical story of the Jewish girl Esther, who became queen and played a heroic role during a conspiracy against her newly wedded husband, is about the intrigues of the ego that likes to claim the throne for itself and can become an obstacle to the sacred marriage.

The name Esther closely resembles Ishtar, a goddess from the pantheon of ancient Babylon, which is an association that a reader in that time certainly would have made. Ishtar was revered as the bringer of the life force (read: the kundalini energy). One of her attributes is a staff along which two serpents spiral. On the image, we see Ishtar in a dress with seven horizontal layers, which is a reference to the seven chakras that the kundalini passes on its way to the crown.

*A terracotta relief depicting the goddess Ishtar.*
*The Louvre, Paris, early 2nd millennium BC.*

The first indication that the entire story of the brave Esther is in fact about an internal process comes as soon as in verse 3 (page 64), where we read that King Ahasuerus, who orders the search for a new partner, lives in a fortress named Susa. The name Susa relates to the Hebrew noun shushan and means lilly, a flower with the same spiritual meaning in the Bible as the lotus has in eastern traditions. Both refer to the process of God-realization. At the chakra level, the flowers are connected with the crown chakra, the place where the physical dimensions and the divine meet and unite.

1   After these things, when the wrath of King Ahasuerus was appeased, he remembered Vashti and what she had done, and what was decreed against her.

2   Then said the king's servants who ministered unto him, "Let there be fair young virgins sought for the king;

3   and let the king appoint officers in all the provinces of his kingdom, that they may gather together all the fair young virgins unto the palace at Shushan, to the house of the women unto the custody of Hegai the king's chamberlain, keeper of the women; and let their things for purification be given them.

4   And let the maiden who pleaseth the king be queen instead of Vashti." And the thing pleased the king, and he did so.

5   Now in the palace at Shushan there was a certain Jew whose name was Mordecai, the son of Jair, the son of Shimei, the son of Kish, a Benjamite,

6   who had been carried away from Jerusalem with the captives who had been carried away with Jeconiah king of Judah, whom Nebuchadnezzar the king of Babylon had carried away.

7   And he brought up Hadassah (that is, Esther), his uncle's daughter; for she had neither father nor mother, and the maid was fair and beautiful, whom Mordecai, when her father and mother were dead, took for his own daughter.

8   So it came to pass, when the king's commandment and his decree were heard, and when many maidens were gathered together unto the palace at Shushan under the custody of Hegai, that Esther was brought also unto the king's house into the custody of Hegai, keeper of the women.

9   And the maiden pleased him, and she obtained kindness from him; and he speedily gave her her things for purification, with such things as belonged to her, and seven maidens who were meet to be given to her out of the king's house; and he preferred her and her maids unto the best place in the house of the women.

10  Esther had not shown her people nor her kindred, for Mordecai had charged her that she should not show it.

11  And Mordecai walked every day before the court of the women's house to know how Esther did and what should become of her.

12  Now when every maid's turn had come to go in to King Ahasuerus, after she had been twelve months according to the manner of the women (for so were the days of their purifications accomplished, to wit, six months with oil of myrrh, and six months with sweet odors and with other things for the purifying of the women),

13  then thus came every maiden unto the king. Whatsoever she desired was given her to go

With the opening verses, the author paints the universal picture of the masculine pole of God (King Ahasuerus) who resides in the crown chakra, and who desires to unite with the feminine pole of God in the pelvis.

From all the girls he is offered, the king choses the pretty virgin Esther. She must endure an intensive and lengthy "beautification procedure" (verses 9 and 12), which represents the purification process that precedes the sacred marriage. This treatment takes no fewer than twelve months, which is a number that refers to spiritual completeness. She is also given at her disposal seven servant girls (chakras) from his house (verse 9).

Esther becomes the new queen and receives a royal crown upon her head (verse 17), which symbolizes the opened crown chakra. The spiritual aspirant who makes it this far now experiences a great inner rest, peace and wealth. This is the meaning of verse 18: *he made a release to the provinces, and gave gifts.*

Two more obstacles need still be removed. In verse 21 we read about two keepers of the door, who seek to lay hands on Ahasuerus and whom the king subsequently has hanged (verse 23). These two men represent the two energy channels that flow along the spinal column and which make a person experience duality. During the sacred marriage these polar energies merge. One might say that they cease to exist, which is symbolized by the hanging of the door keepers.

The gallows upon which the two men die symbolizes the spinal column with the awakened kundalini. The Hebrew source word *etz*, which is here translated with gallows actually means tree. With this choice of words, the author subtly relates to another Biblical tree that also symbolizes the spinal column with an awakened kundalini: the Tree of Life, which stands at the center of Paradise and whose fruits give eternal life (Gen 2:9) - fruits that only come within our reach when the two door keepers (the duality) have been removed.

Later in Esther, in chapter 5, the sacred marriage is sketched once again in graceful imagery:

with her out of the house of the women unto he king's house.

14 In the evening she went, and on the morrow she returned to the second house of the women to the custody of Shaashgaz, the king's chamberlain, who kept the concubines. She
came in unto the king no more unless the king delighted in her and she were called by
name.

15 Now when the turn of Esther, the daughter of Abihail the uncle of Mordecai, who had
taken her for his daughter, had come to go in unto the king, she required nothing but what
Hegai the king's chamberlain, the keeper of the women, appointed. And Esther obtained
favor in the sight of all those who looked upon her.

16 So Esther was taken unto King Ahasuerus into his royal house in the tenth month, which is
the month of Tebeth, in the seventh year of his reign.

17 And the king loved Esther above all the women, and she obtained grace and favor in his
sight more than all the virgins, so that he set the royal crown upon her head, and made
her queen instead of Vashti.

18 Then the king made a great feast unto all his princes and his servants, even Esther's feast;
and he made a release to the provinces, and gave gifts according to the state of the king.

19 And when the virgins were gathered together the second time, then Mordecai sat at the
king's gate.

20 Esther had not yet shown her kindred nor her people, as Mordecai had charged her, for
Esther did the commandment of Mordecai as when she was brought up by him.

21 In those days, while Mordecai sat at the king's gate, two of the king's chamberlains,
Bigthan and Teresh, of those who kept the door, were wroth and sought to lay hands on
King Ahasuerus.

22 And the thing was known to Mordecai, who told it unto Esther the queen, and Esther infor-
med the king thereof in Mordecai's name.

23 And when inquisition was made of the matter, it was found out. Therefore they were both
hanged on a tree, and it was written in the book of the chronicles before the king.
(Esther 2:1-23 KJ21)

*On the third day Esther put on her royal robes and stood in the inner court of the palace, in front of the king's hall. The king was sitting on his royal throne in the hall, facing the entrance.*
*When he saw Queen Esther standing in the court, he was pleased with her and held out to her the gold scepter that was in his hand. So Esther approached and touched the tip of the scepter.*
(Esther 5:1-2)

Esther appears before Ahasuerus and touches the tip of the gold scepter.

The gold scepter represents the spinal column. Esther (the kundalini) travels from the inner court (the pelvis) to the king, who is seated upon his throne (in the crown chakra), and touches the tip of the scepter (the pineal gland at the end of the spinal column).

The royal robes which Esther dons is the incorruptible light-body that is formed during a kundalini process. The "third day," upon which all this takes place, refers to a transformation; symbolism based on the reappearance of the moon after two days of darkness in her cycle.

The final chapters of the Book of Esther are about the intrigues of the grand vizier Haman, who symbolizes the ego. Haman concocts a plan to eradicate all Jews, who represent man's higher nature (see chapter 5). Esther's bold acts lead to Haman's demise on the gallows. This event is still celebrated annually by Jews with the feast of Purim:

*24 because Haman the son of Hammedatha the Agagite, the enemy of all the Jews, had schemed against the Jews to destroy them, and had cast Pur (that is, the lot) to consume them and to destroy them.*
*25 But when Esther came before the king, he commanded by letters that this wicked scheme which Haman devised against the Jews should return upon his own head, and that he and his sons should be hanged on the gallows.*
*26 Therefore they called these days Purim after the name of Pur [that is, Lot]. Therefore for all the words of this letter, and of that which they had seen concerning this matter and what had come upon them,*

*27 the Jews ordained and took upon them and upon their seed and upon all such as joined themselves unto them, that without fail they would keep these two days according to their writing and according to their appointed time every year;*
*28 and that these days should be remembered and kept throughout every generation, every family, every province, and every city, and that these days of Purim should not pass from among the Jews, nor the memorial of them perish from their seed.*
(Esther 9:24-28 KJ21)

Haman's fate is sealed at the moment Esther comes before the king (verse 25): when the kundalini arrives at the sixth chakra, on the forehead, the ego dies.

**The feast of Purim**

A traditional element of the feast of Purim is the eating of a kind of pastry called Haman's Ears. This is a fitting name to celebrate the death of Haman: the sixth chakra, the place where the ego dies, is situated at the height of the ears…!

*Haman's Ears*

# The bent-over woman

In the gospels too we meet women that personify the divine energy in our pelvis. In Luke we read about a bent-over woman, who is healed by Jesus. For eighteen years she had been unable to straighten herself up, which was caused by Satan, says the text (page 70).

A bent-over woman who is unable to "straighten up" (verse 11) is related to the classical metaphor for an inactive or "sleeping" kundalini: a coiled up serpent (the word *kundalini* is Sanskrit and means "coiled", "coiled up" or "coiled up one," which in turn was used to refer to a serpent).

Both Satan and a period of eighteen years (verse 16) point to our lower nature. Satan literally means "opposer." He represents the ego and our animal drives. This "antichrist" (literally "against the anointing") represents everything within us that stands in the way of a process of God-realization.

The number eighteen consists of three times six. In the Book of Revelation we read about 666:

*This calls for wisdom. If anyone has insight, let him calculate the number of the beast, for it is man's number. His number is 666.*
(Revelation 13:18)

For many centuries now, people have speculated who might be referred to with this number. The "number of the beast," however, is not about a specific person. Six represents our lower, animal nature. On the sixth day, God creates both the land animals and man (Genesis 1:24-31). Six, in the Bible, represents the incomplete man, who is connected with his lower nature and has no yet realized his higher nature (seven, the day of God, represents completion, i.e. God-realization).

In Biblical symbolism, a human comprises three aspects: body, feelings and thoughts. Three times six means: body, feelings and thoughts are connected to the animal nature. Said otherwise: the number 666 represents the beast in man.

Jesus lays his hands on the woman and "immediately she was made straight" (verse 13). He causes the kundalini to awaken and she flows upward to the crown.

In the fourth gospel, Mary Magdalene also rises up, twice, to represent the same process, as we will see shortly: at the raising of Lazarus and the resurrection of Jesus.

## The raising of Lazarus

Martha and Mary are the two sisters of the "deceased" Lazarus. Mary personifies the kundalini energy. When Jesus arrives, she, contrary to Martha who goes out to meet Jesus, remains in her house (the pelvis):

*When Martha heard that Jesus was coming, she went out to meet him, but Mary stayed at home.*
(John 11:20)

10 And He was teaching in one of the synagogues on the Sabbath.

11 And behold, there was a woman who had a spirit of infirmity for eighteen years, and was bowed down and could in no way lift herself up.

12 And when Jesus saw her, He called her to Him and said unto her, "Woman, thou art loosed from thine infirmity."

13 And He laid His hands on her, and immediately she was made straight, and glorified God.

14 But the ruler of the synagogue answered with indignation, because Jesus had healed on the Sabbath day, and said unto the people, "There are six days in which men ought to work; in them therefore come and be healed, and not on the Sabbath day."

15 The Lord then answered him and said, "Thou hypocrite! Doth not each one of you on the Sabbath loose his ox or his ass from the stall and lead him away to watering?

16 And ought not this woman, being a daughter of Abraham, whom Satan hath bound, lo, these eighteen years, be loosed from this bond on the Sabbath day?"

17 And when He had said these things, all His adversaries were ashamed; and all the people rejoiced for all the glorious things that were done by Him.

(Luke 13:10-17 KJ21)

Martha then calls her sister, after which Mary rushes toward Jesus:

*And after she had said this, she went back and called her sister Mary aside. "The*
*Teacher is here," she said, "and is asking for you."*
*When Mary heard this, she got up quickly and went to him.*
(John 11:28-29)

This creates the image of the feminine pole of God in the pelvis which rises toward the masculine pole of God in the crown. *"The Master is asking for you…,"* Martha says: the two divine counterpoles in a person desire to unite with each other.

Upon arrival, Maria falls at the feet of Jesus and both begin to weep (John 11:32-35). This is a curious detail. Jesus is about to raise Lazarus. Why would he be crying?
Their tears represent the production of *amrita* in the brain. The pineal gland begins to "weep" under influence of the kundalini energy, which has risen to the head. Opiods are secreted into the brain fluid; a physical aspect of the process of spiritual resurrection.

**Anointing rituals** refer, at a deeper level, to the transformation of the brain fluid into *amrita* during a kundalini awakening. When kings and priests are anointed with oil, this symbolizes the inner spiritual process by which a person becomes an anointed one as a result of the changes in the cerebrospinal fluid (CSF) - a ritual that is a remnant from a time when for royalty or priesthood men and women were selected who were indeed connected with the divine.

Also the anointing that a believer of the Catholic tradition receives upon his or her confirmation stems from this. With his thumb, the priest places a cross of holy *chrism* (consecrated oil) upon the forehead of the confirmand; the location of the sixth chakra, where the merging of the energy channels takes place, which is the energetic commencement of the process of inner "anointing."

*JJan Joest van Calcar*
*Raising of Lazarus, 1506-1508*
*Katholischen Pfarrkirche St. Nikolai, Kalkar*

*Jesus raises Lazarus with the sign of the sacred marriage (2 fingers held together; see page 84).*

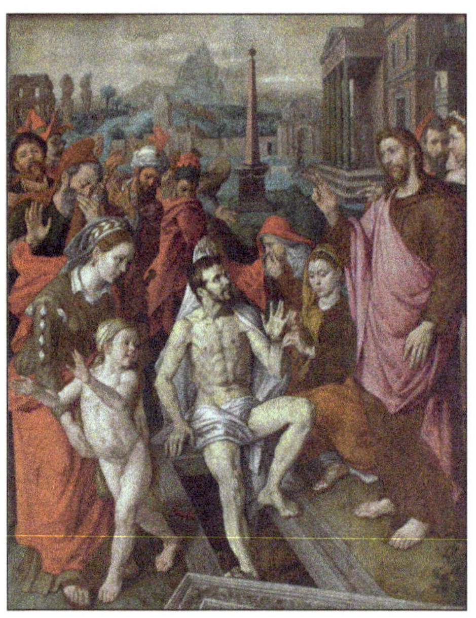

*Jan Cornelisz Vermeyen*
*Raising of Lazarus, 1547-1549*
*Royal Museums of Fine Arts of Belgium, Brussels*

*Jesus and Lazarus both make the sign of the sacred marriage (2 fingers held together). Behind Lazarus stands a pillar, which symbolizes the spinal column with at its top the pineal gland (also see pages 40 and 41).*
*In the foreground to the left, a naked child walks away from the grave, symbolizing the new man who has risen. On the sleeve of the child's mother we see a reference to the caduceus.*

*Nicolas Froment, Raising of Lazarus, 1461*
*Galleria degli Uffizi, Florence, Italy*

*With both hands, Jesus makes the sign of the sacred marriage (2 fingers held together). The white shawl that is tied around the hat of the man to the right, depicts the kundalini that flows upward and activates the pineal gland (the knot in the shawl).*

*Michael Pachter, Raising of Lazarus, 1481*
*Wallfahrtskirche St. Wolfgang im Salzkammergut, Austria.*

*Lazarus lies in his grave in between two large pillars, symbolizing the two energy channels that merge during a spiritual awakening. Jesus makes the sign of the sacred marriage (the joining of these two pillars).*
*The pattern on the ceiling refers to the seven chakras.*

The word Messiah stems from the Hebrew *mashiach* and means anointed. The Greek word for this is Christos. It is a title which, to many, is inseparably connected to Jesus of Nazareth: Jesus the Christ. Every person, however, possess the potential to become a Messiah, an anointed, a Christ![8]

## The anointing of Jesus

The so-called inner "anointing," is depicted again, in a scene that describes a visit of Jesus to the raised Lazarus and his two sisters, and prominently features Mary Magdalene. When they recline to have dinner, Mary anoints the feet of Jesus and dries them with her hair:

*Six days before the Passover, Jesus arrived at Bethany, where Lazarus lived, whom Jesus had raised from the dead.*
*Here a dinner was given in Jesus' honor. Martha served, while Lazarus was among those reclining at the table with him.*
*Then Mary took about a pint of pure nard, an expensive perfume; she poured it on Jesus' feet and wiped his feet with her hair. And the house was filled with the fragrance of the perfume.*
(John 12:1-3)

It was not customary to wipe off the costly oil after an anointing; people simply left it where it was. However, this detail of wiping with hair creates the symbolism of an anointing "from feet to hair" or in other words: from head to toe: of the entire person. This interpretation is confirmed by what follows: *the house was filled with the fragrance of the perfume.* A house symbolizes the person.[9] The message to us is repeated once more: the entire person is (innerly) anointed. Here too Mary and Jesus represent the feminine and masculine aspect within a person, which unite with each other in the sacred marriage; the merger that leads to the inner anointing.

*School of Allgäu, Christ in the House of Simon, 1470-1480, private collection.*

*While Mary Magdalene anoints his feet, Jesus points with two fingers, the sign of the sacred marriage, to an almond-shaped dish containing two fish. This dish with fish refers to the vesica piscis, the classical symbol of the merger of opposites. On the table are seven dishes (chakras).*

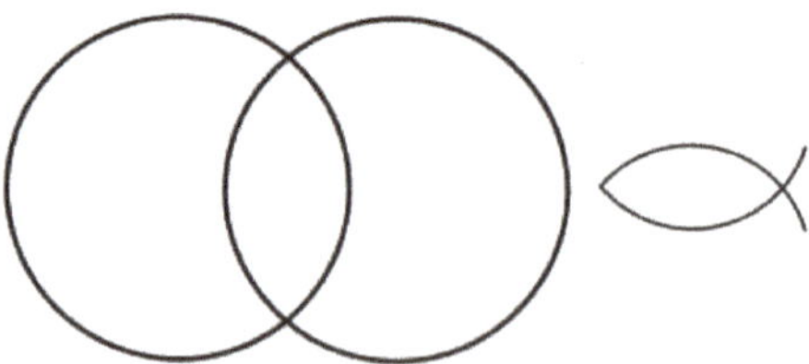

*Jesus in the House of Mary and Martha, unknown artist.*

*On the skirt of Mary we see a reference to the pineal gland.*
*Jesus points toward Mary and to a picture of two persons, one of which wears a crown. In Alchemy, the unification of the divine poles of a person is expressed by the union of king and queen. In the gospels, Jesus and Mary take on the roles of inner king and queen.*

*Image from Alchemy*

11 But Mary stood outside at the sepulcher weeping, and as she wept she stooped down and looked into the sepulcher,

12 and saw two angels in white, sitting one at the head and the other at the feet where the body of Jesus had lain.

13 And they said unto her, "Woman, why weepest thou?" She said unto them, "Because they have taken away my Lord, and I know not where they have laid Him."

14 And when she had thus said, she turned around and saw Jesus standing, and knew not that it was Jesus.

15 Jesus said unto her, "Woman, why weepest thou? Whom seekest thou?" She, supposing Him to be the gardener, said unto Him, "Sir, if thou have borne Him hence, tell me where thou hast laid Him, and I will take Him away."

16 Jesus said unto her, "Mary!" She turned herself and said unto Him, "Rabboni!" (which is to say, "Master").

17 Jesus said unto her, "Touch Me not, for I am not yet ascended to My Father; but go to My brethren and say unto them, 'I ascend unto My Father and your Father, and to My God and your God.'"

18 Mary Magdalene came and told the disciples that she had seen the Lord, and that He had spoken these things unto her.

(John 20:11-18 KJ21)

# Jesus' appearance to Mary Magdalene

The appearance of risen Jesus to Mary Magdalene, who visits his tomb, is moving and full of meaning. This event is described most elaborately in the fourth gospel. Now that we know that Mary is its author, it becomes nothing but logical that she didn't sum up this encounter in a few words, as did the other evangelists. All details were carefully chosen to tell us how we should interpret the resurrection.

During his lifetime, Jesus obtained an immortal light-body: the result of a completed kundalini process. In him, the two divine counterpoles united, and he became one with God the Father: *I and the Father are one* (John 10:30). While still alive, he returned to the Paradise from which Adam and Eve were expelled. He was a "master builder" and, like King Solomon before him, has made of himself an indestructible temple, to which physical death had no claim. All these aspects, Mary incorporated in the eight verses in which she described her encounter with him.

## Mary turns around

That we should see the resurrection as the finale of a kundalini process is expressed by Mary's bodily movements. The hidden symbolism appears when we read the text carefully. First Mary stoops down and looks into the tomb (verse 11). By the stooping down of Mary and the word "into" appears the image of the kundalini energy that is "coiled" up in the tomb of the pelvis.

When Mary comes back up again, she turns twice to Jesus (verses 14 and 16). This is confusing: why does she turn twice? This does not agree with our sense of logic. It is the intention of the author that this draws our attention, because her turning-movements have an important deeper meaning: she is depicting the "kundalini serpent" that spirals upward to the crown.

We see in the Bible frequently a circular movement to describe the rising kundalini. With the fall of Jericho, for instance, when God instructs the priests to walk around the city seven times, carrying the Ark of the Covenant (also see chapter 5). With King Solomon, who builds winding stairs in his temple (1 Kings 6:8). With Samson, who is made to walk in circles to drive a grindstone

(Judges 16:21). Miriam, the sister of Moses and Aaron, performs a whirl-dance after the Israelites crossed the Red Sea on dry land. This whirl-dance, or *mahol* (from the verb *hul*, to whirl), is still performed by Jews during feasts and festivals.

Not only the kundalini energy but also the two energy channels that connect a person with duality, move in spirals upward, along the spinal column to the head. The traditional hair style of orthodox (Hasidic) Jews refers to this: two curly strands of hair at both sides of the head. These so-called *payot* grow from the temples: the level at which the two energy channels merge during the sacred marriage.

## The gardener

Mary first doesn't recognize Jesus and thinks he is the gardener (verse 15). This refers to the Garden of Eden, the Paradise from the Book of Genesis: *The Lord God took the man and put him in the Garden of Eden to work it and take care of it* (Genesis 2:15).

With the image of a gardener, Maria wants to let us know that Jesus is situated in Paradise, i.e. the Kingdom of God, as he calls it himself in the gospels.

## Rabboni

When Maria does recognize Jesus she exclaims: *Rabboni*! She also gives us the translation of that word: Master (verse 16).

Rabboni as appellation of Jesus occurs only twice in the gospels, namely in John 20:16 and Mark 10:51. In by far the most instances (fifteen times), Jesus is called Rabbi, which means Master or Teacher. In the fourth gospel, Mary herself uses Rabbi eight times and once *Rabboni*.

*Rabboni* closely resembles *rab-bani*, which means master-builder. To understand the spiritual meaning of Rabboni we must go to the Book of First Kings, to Solomon's temple. The building of this famous temple is a metaphor for a person who makes him- or herself a temple, for God to live in[10].

In her gospel, Maria has Jesus use the image of the (re-)building of a temple, when he speaks about his future resurrection:

*Jesus answered them, "Destroy this temple, and I will raise it again in three days."*
*The Jews replied, "It has taken forty-six years to build this temple, and you are going to raise it in three days?"*
*But the temple he had spoken of was his body.*
(John 2:19-21)

There are several clues that the temple of Solomon was not a physical building; among others the remarkable fact that during the building no sounds of tools were heard:

*In building the temple, only blocks dressed at the quarry were used, and no hammer, chisel or any other iron tool was heard at the temple site while it was being built.*
(1 Kings 6:7)

The temple was built in seven years, a reference to the seven chakras. For the interior, Hiram was enlisted:

*13 King Solomon sent to Tyre and brought Hiram,*
*14 whose mother was a widow from the tribe of Naphtali and whose father was a man of Tyre and a craftsman in bronze. Hiram was highly skilled and experienced in all kinds of bronze work. He came to King Solomon and did all the work assigned to him.*
(1 Kings 7:13-14)

The name Hiram is a contraction of hara (to burn) and ram (to rise up), and refers to the rising kundalini fire. In the Book of Chronicles he is called Huram-Abi (2 Chronicles 4:16). The added part Ab means Father, so that the meaning of the name becomes: *"Rising fire of the Father."*

Hiram was full of wisdom (read: the kundalini) and was the son of a widow (verse 14). In some traditions and myths, the kundalini energy is seen as a widow as long as she is not united with her masculine pole in the crown chakra. One of the names of the Egyptian goddess Isis, for instance, is "the black widow."

Naphtali, the tribe of the mother of Hiram, comes from the Hebrew *patal*, which means to turn: the motion the kundalini energy makes when she rises.

In the tradition of Freemasonry, the character of Hiram plays a prominent role. As master builder of Solomon, he is seen as an example of the spiritual seeker who wants to make him- or herself into a temple of God. Strictly speaking, not Hiram is the master builder but his employer Solomon. Hiram personifies the kundalini energy who accommodates the renovation of the person. He represents the divine help which Solomon received.

With her exclamation *Rabboni* - Master builder - Mary Magdalene wants to let us know that Jesus too, just like king Solomon, has completed the building of a spiritual temple, with which he has conquered death.

## Son of David

The other time that Jesus is called *Rabboni* is in the gospel of Mark. A blind beggar calls in desperation to Jesus as he walks by:

> *Then they came to Jericho. And as He was leaving Jericho with His disciples and a large crowd, a blind beggar named Bartimaeus, the son of Timaeus, was sitting by the road. When he heard that it was Jesus the Nazarene, he began to cry out and say, "Jesus, **Son of David**, have mercy on me!" Many were sternly telling him to be quiet, but he kept crying out all the more, "**Son of David**, have mercy on me!" And Jesus stopped and said, "Call him here." So they *called the blind man, saying to him, "Take courage, stand up! He is calling for you." Throwing aside his cloak, he jumped up and came to Jesus. And answering him, Jesus said, "What do you want Me to do for you?" And the blind man said to Him, "**Rabboni**, I want to regain my sight!" And Jesus said to him, "Go; your faith has made you well." Immediately he regained his sight and began following Him on the road.*
> (Mark 10:46-52, NAS)

The beggar calls Jesus *Rabboni* and *Son of David*. The son of King David was Solomon. This way, Jesus is also in this passage associated with King Solomon, the Master-builder.

### The name Mary

Also Jesus' exclamation "Mary!" (verse 16) has a deeper meaning. In the source text he uses the Hebrew version of her name: Mariam.
Mariam stems probably from the Egyptian *meri*, which means beloved. This evokes associations with the desired bride from the Song of Solomon, who, as we saw earlier, symbolizes the divine bride or in other words: the kundalini.

Jesus' exclamation "Mariam!" is followed by images that symbolize the completion of the sacred marriage, as we shall see now.

### "Do not hold on to me…"

After Mary has turned to him twice, Jesus says to her: "Do not hold on to me…" (verse 17). Why does Jesus not want Mary to hold on to him? In the gospel of Matthew he is not bothered at all when the astonished women grab hold of their master:

> *Suddenly Jesus met them. "Greetings," he said. They came to him, clasped his feet and worshiped him.*
> (Matthew 28:9)

Mary wants to depict the sacred marriage in her gospel but cannot do that with an embrace. A woman who publicly falls on a man's neck would be deemed highly inappropriate in that time. It would have diminished the glorious image of the resurrected Christ. With the genius insertion of Jesus' rejection: "*do not hold on to me…*" our retina is imprinted by the image of a man and a woman in a passionate embrace. The feminine pole of God (Mary) has straightened herself up from her crouched position with a circular motion, and now unites with the masculine pole of God (Jesus).

**The sign of the sacred marriage**
In Christian iconography, Jesus is often depicted with his index finger and middle finger raised. This gesture is commonly explained as blessing, but its origin and meaning are entirely obscure.

The remaining hidden symbology in art clears up this mystery: the two raised fingers express the merger of opposites. This gesture is supposed to make clear to us that Jesus made the two (energy channels) into one (the kundalini flowing in the spine). Said otherwise: the masculine and the feminine in him have merged. The duality has been transformed into oneness. In him the sacred marriage has taken place. Also see pages 85, 86, 87.

*Jesus said to them, "**When you make the two one**, and when you make the inside like the outside and the outside like the inside, and the above like the below, and when you make the male and the female one and the same, so that the male not be male nor the female female*
*… then will you enter the kingdom."*
Gospel of Thomas, 22

Also with depictions of the encounter between Jesus and Mary Magdalene, gestures are lavishly utilized to convey the deeper meaning of the resurrection from the dead. We see the resurrected Jesus who, with one or two fingers, points toward the forehead of Mary Magdalene. With this the artist wants to tell us: here, inside the head of a person, the resurrection, as a consequence of the sacred marriage, takes place! See pages 88 and 89.

## Jesus makes the sign of the sacred marriage

a.

b.

c.

d.

a. *Gaspard Isenmann.*
b. *Unknown artist, Musée national du Moyen Âge, circa 1500.*
c. *Giovanni da Milano, circa 1365-1369.*
d. *Mariotto di Nardo, 1390-1420.*

e.

f.

g.

e. *Alonso López de Herrera (attr.), first half 17th century.*
f. *Pellegrino di Mariano Rossini, 15th century.*
g. *Niccolò di Pietro Gerini, circa 1390, Santa Felicita, Florence, Italy.*

h.

i.

j.

k.

h. Luis de Morales, 1566.
i. Juan Correa de Vivar, 1540.
j. Maerten de Vos, 1570.
k. Gebhard Fugel, 1893-1894.

## Maria Magdalena encounters the resurrected Jesus

a.
b.
c.
d.

a. *Lucas van Leyden, 1519.*
b. *Bramantino, 1490-1495.*
c. *Albrecht Dürer, 1509-1511.*
d. *Eustache Le Sueur, 1616-1655.*

e.  *Sperindio Cagnola, first half 15th century.*
f.  *Jacob Cornelisz van Oostsanen, 1507*
g.  *André Abellon, 15th century.*

# 4

# The fourth gospel

*And he said, "Whoever finds the interpretation of these sayings will not experience death."*

The Gospel of Thomas, 1

Mary Magdalene not only accompanied Jesus for years, she was also an expert in lived experience in regards to the Kingdom of God. It doesn't surprise, therefore, that the fourth gospel is much more mystical than the synoptic gospels. In this chapter we will have a look at a number of passages and quotes which are found only in the fourth gospel. What information about Mary Magdala and spiritual lessons about the Kingdom of God lay hidden in the symbolism?

# John the Baptist became Jesus the Christ

In writing her gospel, Mary Magdalene not only faced the challenge of hiding her own identity whilst simultaneously leaving clues to retrieve it, but also to both hide and reveal the true identity of Jesus.

Jesus, namely, was during his life known as John the Baptist; a shocking assertion of which I wrote in the book *John the Baptist who became Jesus the Christ*.[11] When he had died, his disciples honored him with a new name and a continued identity, and so showed their contemporaries that John had been, and continued to be, the long awaited Messiah.

John became a Christos, an anointed, after a long process of God-realization. In all gospels, this moment is depicted symbolically by the baptism of Jesus by John in the Jordan. To be recognized by the Jewish people as the Redeemer, John had to fulfill a great number of prophesies from the Jewish Holy Scriptures. As *Joshua, the Son of God*, and with a new identity, as described in the gospels, he met the ideal of the Jews.

### *The Word that had become flesh*

At multiple points in the fourth gospel we find John-is-Jesus clues. First of all in the poetic opening verses about the Word of God (page 94).
According to the traditional, Christian interpretation of this text, John the Baptist was sent by God to witness of the coming of Jesus the Christ, the Son of God.

But the opening words may also mean that John came to witness of the light from God that lived in him. He was the Christ, but the world did not understand him.

## The Word that had become flesh

1   In the beginning was the Word, and the Word was with God, and the Word was God.

2   He was with God in the beginning.

3   Through him all things were made; without him nothing was made that has been made.

4   In him was life, and that life was the light of all mankind.

5   The light shines in the darkness, and the darkness has not overcome it.

6   There was a man sent from God whose name was John.

7   He came as a witness to testify concerning that light, so that through him all might believe.

8   He himself was not the light; he came only as a witness to the light.

9   The true light that gives light to everyone was coming into the world.

10 He was in the world, and though the world was made through him, the world did not recognize him.

11 He came to that which was his own, but his own did not receive him.

12 Yet to all who did receive him, to those who believed in his name, he gave the right to become children of God

13 children born not of natural descent, nor of human decision or a husband's will, but born of God.

14 The Word became flesh and made his dwelling among us. We have seen his glory, the glory of the one and only Son, who came from the Father, full of grace and truth.

15 (John testified concerning him. He cried out, saying, "This is the one I spoke about when I said, 'He who comes after me has surpassed me because he was before me.'")

16 Out of his fullness we have all received grace in place of grace already given.

17 For the law was given through Moses; grace and truth came through Jesus Christ.

18 No one has ever seen God, but the one and only Son, who is himself God and is in closest relationship with the Father, has made him known.

(John 1:1-18)

The text is riddled with subtle clues that support this interpretation. First of all, the name Jesus is mentioned only once, in the penultimate verse. The first sixteen verses are centered on the name John, and his name is mentioned no fewer than three times.

When we reorganize the text somewhat, the intention of the evangelist becomes even more clear:

> *5 … and the darkness has not overcome it.*
> *6 There was a man sent from God whose name was John.*
> *7 He came as a witness to testify concerning that light…*
> *9 The true light that gives light to everyone was coming into the world.*
> *10 … the world did not recognize him.*
> *11 … his own did not receive him.*
> *15 John testified concerning him. He cried out, saying, "This is the one I spoke about when I said, 'He who comes after me has surpassed me because he was before me.'"*

John came to bear witness of the light of God that lived in him; of the Source of our creation (*…He was before me*; verse 15). After an intensive process of purification and emptying, the ego of John made way for God (*He who comes after me…*).

The author places much emphasis on the misjudgment of John: *…has not understood it* (verse 5), *… did not recognize him* (verse 10), *… did not receive him* (verse 11). This explains the change of identity that the evangelists ascribed to John posthumously. Someone who wasn't recognized in life, and subsequently dies a humiliating death on a cross, has little chance to be recognized anyway as the Messiah, the redeemer of the Jews.

The followers of John, who did recognize him, he initiated into the spiritual path that he himself had taken: *Yet to all who received him, to those who believed in his name, he gave the right to become children of God - children born not of natural descent, nor of human decision or a husband's will, but born of God* (verses 12 and 13).

This is confirmed by a more accurate translation of verse 14. The Greek source word *"en"* that is translated with "among" would more properly be translated as "in": *The Word became flesh and made his dwelling **in** us.*

*Diego de Sanabria, Saint John of the Cross, early 16ᵗʰ century, Museo Nacional de Arte, Mexico City, Mexico.*

*John the Baptist is depicted in an unusual way: kneeling in front of a cross. He resembles Jesus. The Ecce Agnes Dei banner is curled around his staff like a serpent. The flower arrangements have the pine cone shape of the pineal gland. John is Jesus.*

Loosely translated, the evangelist says in verse 14: *God became flesh in John and lived also in us.*

The disciples received from John the Holy Spirit; they were baptized by him with the kundalini fire that was flowing through his spinal column in full vehemence:
*From the fullness of his grace we have all received one blessing after another.* (Verse 16).

With this, they received the ability to also become a "One and Only child of God," just like John. The Greek *monogenes*, which traditionally is translated as "only begotten" and the New International Version interprets as "One and Only," and which commonly is understood to mean the only son of God, could also be translated as "born one" or "born unified" and interpreted to refer to a person who has transcended duality and was born (again) in the oneness of the divine.

Interpreted this way, the opening statements of this gospel match perfectly what we know of Mary Magdalene from the Bible stories: that she was inaugurated by Jesus (freed of seven demons; Mark 16:9), and that her spiritual level was revered by the followers of Jesus ("the Tower of God").

## The baptism

Also of great significance is that in the fourth gospel, Jesus isn't baptized by John, as in the other gospels. Here we only read that John saw the Holy Spirit descend:

> *John testified saying, "I have seen the Spirit descending as a dove out of heaven, and He remained on Him."*
> (John 1:32 NAS)

Deliberately, the evangelist doesn't mention the name Jesus but merely speaks of "him," because the descent of the Holy Spirit is about John himself.

John the Baptist points with two fingers (the sign of the sacred marriage) to the head of Jesus: here, in the head, the baptism with the Holy Spirit takes place!

a. Hans Baldun, 1520,
Historisches Museum, Frankfurt am Main

b. Martin Schongauer, 15$^{th}$ century,
Metropolitan Museum of Art, New York City.

The long cloth with knot around Jesus' waist symbolizes the kundalini that flows to the pineal gland. Also the fleur-de-lys in the aureole of Jesus symbolizes the pineal gland (see appendix 1).

c. Master of Frankfurt, 1500-1520,
Museu Nacional d'Art de Catalunya,
Barcelona, Spain.

d. Wolf Traut, 1517,
Germanisches National Museum,
Nuremberg, Germany.

The dark blue iris in the lower left corner of
the painting represents a process of kundalini
awakening (see appendix 1).

When we change the punctuation of this text somewhat - the Greek source text has no interpunction - we could also read this quote as:

*Then John gave this testimony: "I saw the Spirit come down from heaven as a dove." And He [the Spirit] remained on him [John].*

It hurts Maria noticeably more than the other evangelists that she cannot write the truth about John. Likewise, the authors of the synoptic gospels left clues in their writing that John was Jesus[12], but they took less effort than Mary to approach the truth as closely as possible.

We see this also at the moment that John the Baptist exits the stage in the gospels, to make way for Jesus. In the synoptic gospels, John is imprisoned and subsequently decapitated by Herod (a decapitation is a metaphor for the death of the ego)[13]. The fourth gospel merely speaks of John's imprisonment, after which he doesn't reappear in the text (John 3:23-24).

## Disciple of John the Baptist

Another noteworthy detail that jumps out when we read the fourth gospel is that the author consequently refers to John the Baptist as simply John. Nowhere occurs his epithet Baptist. This fits someone who knew John closely. Someone like Mary Magdalene.

In continuation of our conclusion that she is the author of the fourth gospel, we can deduce from the text that she had been a disciple of John/Jesus before the twelve men we know as the apostles. In the following passage, she describes how the first disciples join him:

**The first disciples**
*35 The next day John was there again with two of his disciples.*
*36 When he saw Jesus passing by, he said, "Look, the Lamb of God!"*
*37 When the two disciples heard him say this, they followed Jesus.*
*38 Turning around, Jesus saw them following and asked, "What do you want?"*
*They said, "Rabbi" (which means "Teacher"), "where are you staying?"*

*39 "Come," he replied, "and you will see." So they went and saw where he was staying, and they spent that day with him. It was about four in the afternoon.*
*40 Andrew, Simon Peter's brother, was one of the two who heard what John had said and who had followed Jesus.*
*41 The first thing Andrew did was to find his brother Simon and tell him, "We have found the Messiah" (that is, the Christ).*
(John 1:35-41)

Verse 35 speaks of "two disciples" of John the Baptist. In verse 41 we learn that one of these two disciples is called Andrew. The identity of the second person remains unclear. Why is everybody called by name except this second disciples? Because it is the author of the gospel, and she has to remain anonymous: Mary Magdalene!

Judging from her own words, Mary was thus not simply one of the woman who followed Jesus on his travels (Matthew 27:55-56, Mark 15:40-41, Luke 8:1-3). She belonged to his very first disciples and probably closely experienced the transformation of the prophet John into the enlightened man Jesus.

The English translation of verse 39 mentions "four in the afternoon," but the Greek original speaks of "tenth hour." The "tenth hour" refers to the spiritual state of Jesus, or "where he was staying." The number ten, two whole hands, represents perfection or completion in the Bible; a state of wholeness, to which Jesus also incited his disciples:

*Be perfect, therefore, as your heavenly Father is perfect.*
(Matthew 5:48)

The Greek *teleios*, from the quote above, means perfect in the sense of fully made, fully whole, fully completed, fully grown.

Jesus is the completed man John. This explains why the two disciples switch masters so impulsively, even when they merely observed Jesus from a small distance. In reality, the disciples remained with the same teacher, who only (on paper) changed identity.

*Johann Georg Bergmüller, 1741, Pfarrkirche, Steingaden, Germany.*

*Judging from their attributes, on the cloud are seated John the Baptist and John the Evangelist. John the Baptist (left) strongly resembles Jesus and the evangelist looks like a woman. With this the artist wants to let us know: these are Jesus and Mary Magdalene!*

### *The arrest of Jesus*

The character of the mysterious, nameless disciple, Mary also deploys in the account of the arrest of Jesus:

*Simon Peter and another disciple were following Jesus. Because this disciple was known to the high priest, he went with Jesus into the high priest's courtyard, but Peter had to wait outside at the door. The other disciple, who was known to the high priest, came back, spoke to the girl on duty there and brought Peter in.*
(John 18:15-16)

This time too it's probable that the anonymous disciple is Mary Magdalene herself. Also because in the synoptic gospels Peter alone goes with Jesus to the high priest.

Ossuary of Miriam,
granddaughter of Caiaphas.

**The ossuary of Miriam**
In June 2011, archeologists discovered an ossuary (a box to store someone's skeletal remains), with inscribed on it: Miriam, daughter of Yeshua, son of Caiaphas, priest of Ma'aziah of Beth 'Imri.
Miriam is the Hebrew version of the name Maria.
The author of the fourth gospel writes that the anonymous disciple was allowed in with Jesus because this disciple was known to the high priest (John 18:16).
The name of this high priest was Caiaphas (John 18:13).
The discovery of the ossuary gave rise to the intriguing hypothesis that Mary Magdalene was allowed into the palace with Jesus because she was the granddaughter of Caiaphas (and that the ossuary of Mary Magdalene was recovered)!

## Mary Magdalene versus Peter

Something else that jumps out when we study the fourth gospel is that the apostle Peter isn't shown in a very good light. He is mentioned far fewer times than in the synoptic gospels, and when he appears, he is depicted as ignorant or disloyal. Let's have a look at the passages in question:

### The last supper

Jesus lays at the dinner table with his disciples, on the eve of his crucifixion. To the great consternation of all present, he announces that he will be betrayed by one of them. When Peter wants to know who that might be, he solicits the help of the author:

> *One of them, the disciple whom Jesus loved, was reclining next to him. Simon Peter motioned to this disciple and said, "Ask him which one he means."*
> (John 13:23-24)

Peter, apparently, can't or won't ask this himself of Jesus but inquires of the person who occupies the place of honor during the dinner: reclining at the bosom of Jesus. With this passage the authors indicates to be closer to Jesus than Peter.

### The betrayal of Peter

Also in other situations in which Peter appears on the stage, he has to be helped by the author. The second time is at Jesus' arrest (John 18:15-27). When he is lead into the palace of the high priest, Peter must remain outside, but a few moments later, the anonymous other disciple - Mary Magdalene - arranges that he is allowed inside.

In this passage we also read that three times Peter denies to be a disciple of Jesus (the synoptic gospels report the same). The golden rooster on the steeple of Catholic churches are supposed to remind us of this shameful event.

### The crucifixion and the empty grave

At the crucifixion, only women, including Mary Magdalene, are present. The male disciples have fled. The empty tomb is first discovered by Mary Magdalene. Peter and another disciple, who isn't named, are called to the scene by her (John 20:1-3). These are two crucial events for the Christian faith, in which Peter remains in the shadow of Mary Magdalene.

## The resurrection

According to three of the four gospels, the resurrected Jesus appears first to Mary Magdalena and he instructs her to deliver the good news to the other disciples. Only the evangelist Luke has Jesus appear to the male disciples, among whom Peter.

## The appearance at the Sea of Tiberias

In the final chapter, the author of the fourth gospel clarifies once again how things relate. Jesus appears to a number of his disciples at the Sea of Tiberias (John 21:1-14). They don't recognize him immediately. In verse 7, a penny drops:

> *Then the disciple whom Jesus loved said to Peter, "It is the Lord!" As soon as Simon Peter heard him say, "It is the Lord," he wrapped his outer garment around him (for he had taken it off) and jumped into the water.*
> (John 21:7)

The author recognizes Jesus and explains (again) to Peter what's going on. A few verses on, Peter is told by Jesus not to concern himself with the plans Jesus has with the author:

> *Peter turned and saw that the disciple whom Jesus loved was following them. (This was the one who had leaned back against Jesus at the supper and had said, "Lord, who is going to betray you?")*
> *When Peter saw him, he asked, "Lord, what about him?"*
> *Jesus answered, "If I want him to remain alive until I return, what is that to you? You must follow me."*
> (John 21:20-22)

## The gospel of Thomas

Mary Magdalene did not have the same warm connection with Peter as she had with Jesus. Her gospel bulges with clues that there was great tension between these two important disciples.

In the apocryphal (extra-Biblical) gospel of Thomas, we can read Peter's own thoughts on this:

## Jesus Teaches Nicodemus

1 Now there was a Pharisee, a man named Nicodemus who was a member of the Jewish ruling council.

2 He came to Jesus at night and said, "Rabbi, we know that you are a teacher who has come from God. For no one could perform the signs you are doing if God were not with him."

3 Jesus replied, "Very truly I tell you, no one can see the kingdom of God unless they are born again."

4 "How can someone be born when they are old?" Nicodemus asked. "Surely they cannot enter a second time into their mother's womb to be born!"

5 Jesus answered, "Very truly I tell you, no one can enter the kingdom of God unless they are born of water and the Spirit.

6 Flesh gives birth to flesh, but the Spirit gives birth to spirit.

7 You should not be surprised at my saying, 'You must be born again.'

8 The wind blows wherever it pleases. You hear its sound, but you cannot tell where it comes from or where it is going. So it is with everyone born of the Spirit."

9 "How can this be?" Nicodemus asked.

10 "You are Israel's teacher," said Jesus, "and do you not understand these things?

11 Very truly I tell you, we speak of what we know, and we testify to what we have seen, but still you people do not accept our testimony.

12 I have spoken to you of earthly things and you do not believe; how then will you believe if I speak of heavenly things?

13 No one has ever gone into heaven except the one who came from heaven—the Son of Man.

14 Just as Moses lifted up the snake in the wilderness, so the Son of Man must be lifted up,

15 that everyone who believes may have eternal life in him."

16 For God so loved the world that he gave his one and only Son, that whoever believes in him shall not perish but have eternal life.

17 For God did not send his Son into the world to condemn the world, but to save the world through him.

18 Whoever believes in him is not condemned, but whoever does not believe stands condemned already because they have not believed in the name of God's one and only Son.

19 This is the verdict: Light has come into the world, but people loved darkness instead of light because their deeds were evil.

20 Everyone who does evil hates the light, and will not come into the light for fear that their deeds will be exposed.

21 But whoever lives by the truth comes into the light, so that it may be seen plainly that what they have done has been done in the sight of God.

(John 3:1-21)

*Simon Peter said to him, "Let Mary leave us, for women are not worthy of life."
Jesus said, "I myself shall lead her in order to make her male, so that she too may
become a living spirit resembling you males. For every woman who will make
herself male will enter the kingdom of heaven."*
Gospel of Thomas, 114

Such misogyny was not uncommon in that time. But one would expect that a
close disciple of Jesus would have been gradually cured of it. Nowhere in the
Bible stories we find the least trace of sexism with Jesus.
Peter, however, is not a flexible man, as is made evident also by the other three
gospels. He continuously struggles to understand Jesus and strongly protests when
Jesus does something he doesn't like (for example Matt. 16:22 and John 13:8).

## *Power struggle*

What can we conclude from all of this?
That in the early Christian community, there probably was a power struggle
between Mary Magdalene, the most important disciple and confidant of Jesus,
and Peter, the foremost of the apostles. This struggle was evidently concluded
in Peter's favor. Until today, Christians regard Peter as the main founder of their
church, and Maria's position has been marginalized as "one of the women who
followed Jesus."

# The rebirth

The fourth gospel contains a remarkable conversation that Jesus has with the
Pharisee Nicodemus, about the necessity of a rebirth in order to enter the King-
dom of God (see previous page). Neither this conversation, nor the character of
Nicodemus, is mentioned by the other gospels.

The importance of this recorded dialogue can hardly be overestimated. Not
only has this passage (the rebirth) become a pillar of Christian dogma, the
spiritual seeker also obtains crucial clues from Jesus himself about the inner
realization of the Kingdom of God.
In verse 5 (page 106), Jesus says: *"no one can enter the kingdom of God unless he
is born of water and the Spirit."*

*Unknown artist, 1570, National Museum of Ancient Art, Lisbon, Portugal.*

*The rope with which Jesus is bound "spirals" upward like a serpent.*

The meaning of this is that the person first has to undergo a purification process – during which the Holy Spirit transforms the person – before God can take up domicile within us.

In order to explain, Jesus continues in verse 8: "*The wind blows wherever it pleases. You hear its sound, but you cannot tell where it comes from or where it is going. So it is with everyone born of the Spirit.*"

With this he explains what the purification process by the Spirit leads to. The ego is cleansed of all ballast and contamination. It becomes "transparent" and seemingly absent. The reborn person experiences only consciousness, without thoughts. The personal past no longer affects one's emotions. Others experience this person as without ego, as transparent *like the wind*.

In the Book of Isaiah, God explicitly names the erasure of one's personal past:

> *Behold, I will create new heavens*
> *and a new earth.*
> *The former things will not be remembered,*
> *nor will they come to mind.*
> (Isaiah 65:17)

Jesus says that he knows what he is talking about, that he speaks from his own experience (verse 11). He too has gone through this process of rebirth and renounced his ego. What he says comes from God and not from his ego.

The conversation appears to take a different turn when Jesus, in verse 14, announces his crucifixion. But also with these words he elucidates the concept of rebirth.

All evangelists describe the crucifixion of Jesus in such a way that it is a metaphor for the dying of the ego. His resurrection from the dead symbolizes the spiritual rebirth of a person who renounced his ego.[14]

Jesus himself confirms this interpretation by making a connection with the story of Moses and the bronze serpent: *Just as Moses lifted up the snake in the desert, so the Son of Man must be lifted up...* (verse 14). This is a direct reference to a kundalini awakening!

## Moses and the bronze serpent

On their forty year trek through the desert, the people of Moses get to deal with serpents whose bite is deadly. God orders Moses to manufacture a serpent from bronze, and put it up on a pole. Whoever looks upon the bronze serpent after he has been bitten, will survive (Numbers 21:4-9).

The Hebrew that is translated with venomous snake (NIV) or fiery serpent (KJV) is *nahash saraph*, which means burning snake. These snakes of fire represent the kundalini or Holy Spirit. The story shows what the consequences are when the divine energy in the pelvis is engaged for the desires of the underbelly: for the satisfaction of the senses and superfluous pleasure.

When, after awakening, the "fiery serpent" is not guided upward but stagnates in the pelvis, where it sets the belly on fire ("burning with desire"), it will be a deadly poison for the soul. The person dies in the spiritual sense. But if the serpent is guided upward though the spinal column ("put up on a pole"), the person stays "alive."

With his statement that he must be lifted up the way Moses lifted up the serpent, Jesus wants to let us know that we should see his crucifixion as a depiction of a kundalini awakening. He will physically express this inner process of God-realization. He will make the dying of the ego and the inner resurrection visible in the sight of the whole world: a horrible display that makes one wonder if this spiritual lesson could not have been presented in some other way.

In any case, the inhuman suffering and dying of Jesus didn't fail to have effect. It left deep traces in our collective consciousness and made Christianity a world religion.

### The vanishing of Enoch

Becoming invisible, like the wind, has a beautiful parallel in the Old Testament: the story about the vanishing of Enoch. Enoch leads a pious life until, after 365 years, he is "taken away" by God. This story from the Book of Genesis covers a mere four verses:

*When Enoch had lived 65 years, he became the father of Methuselah.*
*After he became the father of Methuselah, Enoch walked faithfully with God 300 years and had other sons and daughters.*
*Altogether, Enoch lived a total of 365 years.*
*Enoch walked faithfully with God; then he was no more, because God took him away.*
(Genesis 5:21-24)

The emptying that is required to obtain the Kingdom of God, a person cannot achieve by his own strength. The ego cannot make itself disappear. For this, a purification process by the Holy Spirit is needed. God "takes us away" when we have made ourself worthy for this by a life dedicated to God (the name Enoch means dedicated).

This also resounds in the letter of the apostle Paul to his fellow worker Titus, in which he speaks of the washing of rebirth and renewal by the Holy Spirit:

*But when the kindness and love of God our Savior appeared, he saved us, not because of righteous things we had done, but because of his mercy, he saved us through the washing of rebirth and renewal by the Holy Spirit, whom he poured out on us generously through Jesus Christ our Savior.*
(Titus 3:4-5)

For a rebirth and a salvation, we depend on God's mercy. This is a message that evokes resistance in the ego, which prefers to regard spiritual advancements as a personal achievement and likes to derive status from it. Many a spiritual seeker plunges into this trap!

*Cristobal de Villalpando, 1683, Moses and the Brazen Serpent and the Transfiguration of Jesus, Cathedral of Puebla, Mexico.*

*In this painting, Moses' serpent has wings, which is an extra-Biblical detail. It's a reference to the caduceus, the symbol of a kundalini awakening.*

*Peter Paul Rubens and studio (ascribed to), Christ with the brazen serpent, 1610-1612, private collection.*

## The Crucifixion of Jesus

17 Carrying his own cross, he went out to the place of the Skull (which in Aramaic is called Golgotha).

18 There they crucified him, and with him two others—one on each side and Jesus in the middle.

19 Pilate had a notice prepared and fastened to the cross. It read: JEZUS OF NAZARET, THE KING OF THE JEWS.

20 Many of the Jews read this sign, for the place where Jesus was crucified was near the city, and the sign was written in Aramaic, Latin and Greek.

21 The chief priests of the Jews protested to Pilate, "Do not write 'The King of the Jews,' but that this man claimed to be king of the Jews."

22 Pilate answered, "What I have written, I have written."

23 When the soldiers crucified Jesus, they took his clothes, dividing them into four shares, one for each of them, with the undergarment remaining. This garment was seamless, woven in one piece from top to bottom.

24 "Let's not tear it," they said to one another. "Let's decide by lot who will get it." This happened that the scripture might be fulfilled that said, "They divided my clothes among them and cast lots for my garment." So this is what the soldiers did.

25 Near the cross of Jesus stood his mother, his mother's sister, Mary the wife of Clopas, and Mary Magdalene.

26 When Jesus saw his mother there, and the disciple whom he loved standing nearby, he said to her, "Woman, here is your son,"

27 and to the disciple, "Here is your mother." From that time on, this disciple took her into his home.

28 Later, knowing that everything had now been finished, and so that Scripture would be fulfilled, Jesus said, "I am thirsty."

29 A jar of wine vinegar was there, so they soaked a sponge in it, put the sponge on a stalk of the hyssop plant, and lifted it to Jesus' lips.

30 When he had received the drink, Jesus said, "It is finished." With that, he bowed his head and gave up his spirit.

(John 19:17-27)

### Living water

Another metaphor for the kundalini energy in the fourth gospel is "living water," which is a term not found in the synoptic gospels.

> *Jesus answered, "Everyone who drinks this water will be thirsty again, but whoever drinks the water I give him will never thirst. Indeed, the water I give him will become in him a spring of water welling up to eternal life."*
> (John 4:13-14)

> *Whoever believes in me, as the Scripture has said, streams of living water will flow from within him. By this he meant the Spirit, whom those who believed in him were later to receive. Up to that time the Spirit had not been given, since Jesus had not yet been glorified.*
> (John 7:38-39)

"A spring of living water which wells up within a person…" With this the author gives a both concrete and poetic description of an inner process that renders *eternal life*.

## The crucifixion

In the succinct description of the crucifixion and burial of Jesus, a true trove of symbolism is inserted. In the imagery that is sketched we find allusions to the sacred marriage, to the caduceus (the staff of Hermes) and the hexagram; all universal symbols of the unification of opposites (the duality) within a person into a (divine) oneness.

A number of elements surrounding the crucifixion are found only in this gospel:
- There are three Mary's at the cross (in the synoptic gospels, none of the disciples are there).
- Jesus instructs the author to take his mother into his home.
- A stalk of the hyssop plant is used to bring wine vinegar to Jesus' mouth.
- Jesus' last words: "*It is finished.*"
- The side of Jesus is pierced with a spear.

An initial clue that we are to interpret the story of Jesus' crucifixion as something that takes place in the head of a person (the dying of the ego, at the level of the sixth chakra), is the name of the place where the crucifixion takes place: the place of the Skull (John 19:17)!

## The caduceus

Several elements in the crucifixion story refer to the caduceus, the staff of the Greek god Hermes (see chapter 1), and with that a kundalini awakening. The two men who are crucified with Jesus - one on each side (verse 18) - depict the two serpents that spiral along the staff. These serpents represent the two energy channels that keep us tethered to the duality, and which merge at the level of the forehead during a spiritual awakening. Symbolically spoken, in the crucifixion story, death occurs to the duality (the two men) and the ego (Jesus).

The stalk of the hyssop plant with the sponge on it, which is brought to the mouth of Jesus to let him drink (verse 29), depicts the staff of the caduceus. The sponge (the knob of the staff) represents the pineal gland.

Bringing the sponge up to the head of Jesus symbolizes the kundalini energy that rises within the spinal column. This interpretation explains the author's choice of the hyssop plant: a relatively small, not very sturdy plant. The authors of the synoptic gospels speak of a reed, which is much more suitable for this function. In that time, the hyssop was known for its healing and purifying effect. In the Old Testament, hyssop is associated with cleaning. In the Psalms, there is even a direct connection made with the effect of the Holy Spirit:

> *Cleanse me with hyssop, and I will be clean; wash me, and I will be whiter than snow.*
> *Let me hear joy and gladness; let the bones you have crushed rejoice.*
> *Hide your face from my sins and blot out all my iniquity.*
> *Create in me a pure heart, O God, and renew a steadfast spirit within me.*
> *Do not cast me from your presence or take your Holy Spirit from me.*
> (Psalm 51:7-11)

Also in the resurrection scene we find references to the caduceus. Mary discovers that the tomb is empty and sees two angels:

*But Mary stood outside the tomb crying. As she wept, she bent over to look into the tomb*
*and saw two angels in white, seated where Jesus' body had been, one at the head and the other at the foot.*
*They asked her, "Woman, why are you crying?" "They have taken my Lord away," she said, "and I don't know where they have put him." At this, she turned around and saw Jesus standing there, but she did not realize that it was Jesus.*
(John 20:11-13)

In none of the other gospels we read of an angel at the head and an angel at the foot of the place *where Jesus' body had been*. When we imagine the wings of the two angels at the head and feet of Jesus, the meaning of this becomes clear: The angels refer to the god Hermes, the owner of the caduceus, who is often depicted with two wings on his helmet and two wings at his feet…!

The gospel of John contains an additional third reference to the caduceus. In chapter 1 we read:

*Then John gave this testimony: "I saw the Spirit come down from heaven as a dove and remain on him.*
(John 1:32)

In all gospels we read that during the baptism, the Holy Spirit "descends like a dove," but only in the fourth gospel he *remains on him*, because of which an image emerges of two wings floating above Jesus' head: a caduceus of flesh and blood!

**Visual art**
Artists too have made use of carefully placed angel wings and other caduceus symbolism to clarify the deeper meaning of the crucifixion story to the audience.

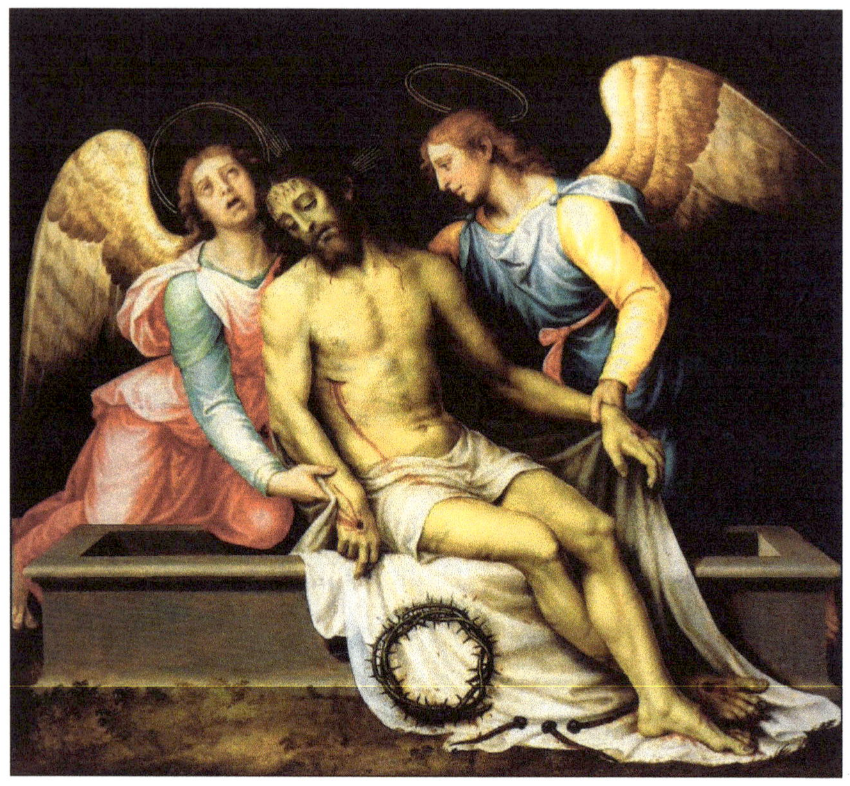

*Juan de Juanes, Pieta Christus Patiens, 1550, Caylus Anticuario, Madrid, Spain.*

*Of the angels only two wings are visible, because of which the image of the caduceus emerges. With his right hand, Jesus makes the sign of the sacred marriage (2=1).*

*Hieronymus Wierix, Allegory on two laws, 1607, Rijksmuseum, Amsterdam, the Netherlands.*

*The vines behind the cross, and the dove of the Holy Spirit above it, remind of the image of the caduceus. With both hands, Jesus makes the sign of the sacred marriage.*

*Hans Baldung, Nativity of Jesus, 1539,*
*Staatliche Kunsthalle, Karlsruhe, Germany.*

*Left and right of the infant Jesus an angel wing is visible, because of which the image of the caduceus is generated. One of the angels points toward the head of Jesus: here the divine birth takes place. With both hands, Mary makes the sign of the sacred marriage.*

## The sacred marriage

The masculine and the feminine in a person merge into oneness when the kundalini energy has arrived at the forehead. This so called sacred marriage is often depicted by the joining of a man and a woman, whether or not in the form of a marriage.

In verse 26 and 27 of the crucifixion scene, *Jesus gives the disciple whom he loved* (the author) the instruction to take his mother into his house. This is a reference to the sacred marriage. The author writes about "himself" in the masculine form. Jesus calls his mother in the fourth gospel consistently "woman" instead of Maria. Likewise in this passage. With this it is emphasized that Jesus' mother, at the symbolic level, embodies the feminine archetype.

In the Greek source text of verse 27, the word "house" does not occur. Literally translated it says: *the disciple took her into his own.* This is a careful selected formulation which is supposed to evoke the image of the sacred marriage.

### Visual art

One of the ways in which artists have incorporated the deeper meaning of the crucifixion in their paintings is to have one of those present in the composition point toward Jesus with two fingers (the sign of the sacred marriage). See page 122.

## The spear

After Jesus on the cross has given up his spirit, a soldier pierces his side with a spear to be sure that he has died (John 19:34). This too is a reference to an inner merger of the polarities, and hails back to the story of Adam and Eve.

Initially there was on earth only the human Adam, living carefree in the Garden of Eden. This paradise is a metaphor for experiencing a living connection with God. God creates Adam androgynous: he is man and woman in one. When God creates for Adam a "helper" and forms Eve from one of his ribs, the consequences are immediate. Eve convinces Adam to eat from the forbidden fruits, and both are expelled from paradise (Genesis 2 and 3). This symbolizes what happens upon the incarnation of a person: he becomes divided into a mascu-

*Agnolo Gaddi, 1390, Museo Nacional Thyssen-Bornemisza, Madrid, Spain.*

*Lucas Cranach the Younger, 1584, Germanisches Nationalmuseum, Nuremberg, Germany.*

*Lucas Cranach the Elder, 1538, Seville Museum of Fine Arts, Seville, Spain.*

*Meister von St. Leonhard, 1450, Salzburg Museum, Austria.*

line and a feminine half, and loses the connection with God. Each times a child is born, the story of Adam and Eve again plays out (internally).[15]

To return to Paradise, a person must return to a state of androgyny. This takes place during the sacred marriage: a person becomes both man and woman in one.
When Jesus hangs on the cross, the spear pierces the same spot where from Adam a rib was taken. Symbolically, with this the rib (Eve) is put back and the state of androgyny is restored.

When Adam and Eve are cast out of paradise, God also punishes the serpent which seduced Eve to eat from the forbidden fruits. He is to crawl on his belly (Genesis 3:14). This symbolizes the kundalini energy that withdraws into the pelvis. The person no longer experiences a living relationship with God.

Jesus "lifted" the serpent "up" again and the images surrounding his crucifixion are to make this clear to us. He is "the new Adam"; an androgynous human who - during his life! - has unified himself with God: *I and the Father are one* (John 10:30).

**Visual art**
One of the methods that artists have used to express the inner process that took place in Jesus is the androgynous person: Jesus with an appearance that balances on the line between masculine and feminine (omitting the usual beard). See page 125.

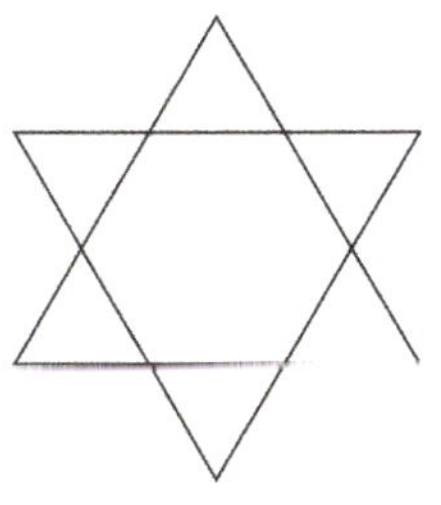

### *The hexagram*
Multiple spiritual traditions feature the symbol of the hexagram, among which Judaism and Hinduism. This six-pointed star comprises two overlapping triangles and expresses the unification of opposites; the sacred marriage.

*Codex Laurentianus, Ashburham 1166, 14th century, Laurentian Library, Florence, Italy.*

*This illustration from the tradition of alchemy shows a tree that grows from the pelvis of a man, who is also shot with an arrow in his side. The tree is the Tree of Life from Paradise as mentioned in Genesis, or in other words: the "kundalini tree," and depicts the divine energy which rises from the pelvis via the spinal column to the crown. The arrow in the side symbolizes, just like the spear with which Jesus is pierced on the cross, the placing back of the rib that was removed from Adam to create Eve. This illustration depicts the end result of the alchemical process: a spiritual awakening (the tree) and a return to the state of androgyny (the arrow). In the left upper quadrant we see the Hand of God, the "director" of this process.*

a. Ciampietrino
b. Leonardo da Vinci
c. Antonio Allegri da Correggio
d. Milanese School, 16th Century

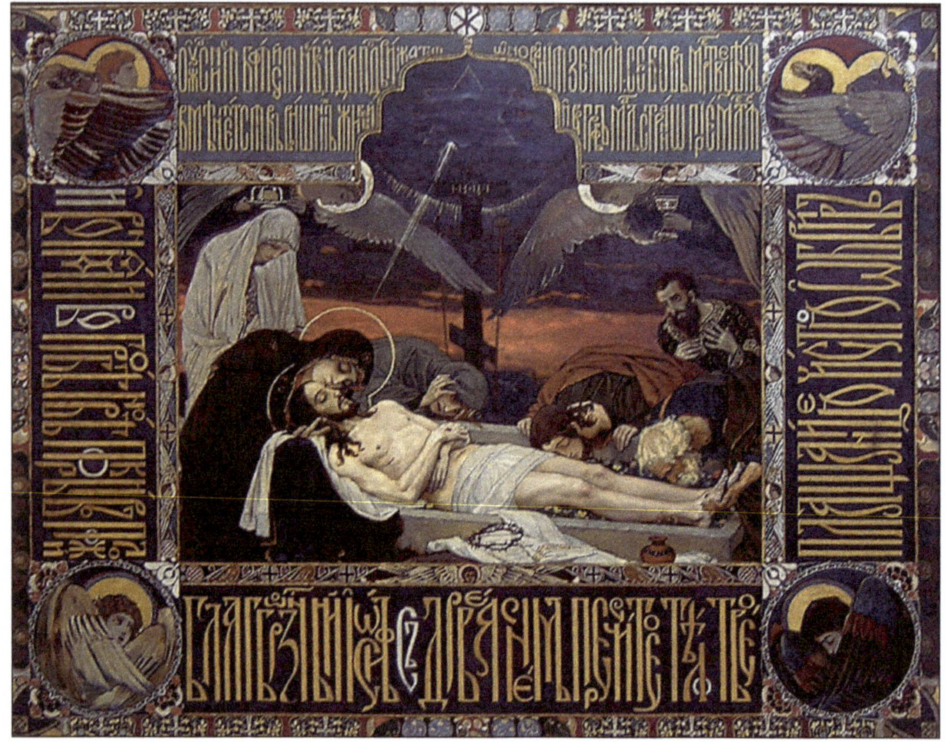

*Viktor Vasnetsov, Entombment of the Christ, 1896,*
*Tretyakov Gallery, Moscow, Russia.*

*From the hexagram, in the top of the picture, a ray of light shines toward the heads of Jesus and Maria. Their aureoles form the vesica piscis; a universal symbol for the merger of opposites (the sacred marriage), just like the hexagram. Mary and Jesus (the feminine and the masculine) symbolize these opposites.*

*Albrecht Altdorfer, Christ on the Cross with Mary and St John, ca 1512, Gemäldegalerie Alte Meister, Kassel, Germany.*

*Beneath the cross we see a hexagram (and unusual detail in crucifixion scenes). With both hands, Jesus makes the sign of the sacred marriage.*
*John has his back toward the viewer. With this the artist wants to let us know that this is someone other than John: Mary Magdalene!*

In the crucifixion scene, a hexagram is hidden in the grouping of those present. For this we must first return to the source text. In verse 25 it seems as if there are four women at the cross. But in reality they are three, and all are named Mary…!

Because it is unlikely that the sister of Jesus' mother was also named Mary, translators started to add commas and words that the source text does not contain, because of which beautiful and essential symbolism has been lost.

The source text of verse 19:25 goes:
*Near the cross of Jesus stood his mother his mother's sister Mary the wife of Clopas and Mary Magdalene.*

The Greek goddess Hecate depicted in triplicate. Marble, Roman copy of an original from the Hellenic period. Museo Chiaramonti, Vatican Museums.

In the presence of the three women, all with the name Mary, shimmers symbolism of the trinity. That is precisely what the evangelist has in mind. In our mind's eye appears a miniature of three crucified men, suspended in the air, and three Mary's standing on the ground: the hexagram displayed in images.

Also with different names, the three men in the air and the three women on the ground a hexagram would have been visible. Three Mary's render the symbolism an extra dimension.

First of all, three women with the same name evokes the image of the "triple goddess," certainly with readers of that time. The phenomenon of goddesses who present themselves in the form of a trinity is found in various spiritual traditions. Inanna, Ishtar and Astarte, from the pantheon of Mesopotamia, for instance. And Hera, Demeter and Aphrodite, from Greek mythology.

In addition to this, the name Mary is also of significance. We saw in chapter 3 that this means "beloved."

Three times "Mary" fortifies the association with the "divine beloved," who was positioned beneath the cross. With Jesus as "Son of God" above, we see the image of the two divine lovers from the Song of Solomon, which yearn to unite with each other.

### The undergarment

That this unification in Jesus has long taken place, the author lets us know in verse 23. The soldiers divide Jesus' outer garments in four parts, which is a reference to the earth (the number four), or in others words: the mortality of his body. His consciousness, however, symbolized by his undergarment, was one with God: woven *in one piece from top to bottom…*

### Mary of Clopas

The name Clopas (verse 26) means traversal or transition. This is no coincidence. Nowhere else in the Bible we read about a Mary of Clopas. Her presence at the cross in the fourth gospel underlines that the grievous death of Jesus is a depiction of a spiritual rebirth, during which the old person "dies".

### Hundred pounds

In the details surrounding the funeral of Jesus we find a second hexagram, namely the mixture with which his dead body is embalmed:

> *Pilate gave him leave. He came therefore and took the body of Jesus. And there came also Nicodemus, who at first came to Jesus by night, and brought a mixture of myrrh and aloes, about a hundred pounds in weight. Then took they the body of Jesus and wound it in linen cloths with the spices, as is the manner of the Jews for burial.*
> (John 19:38-40 KJ21)

A hundred pounds of balsam is an outrageously large quantity. Of course these were Roman pounds, but they still would have added up to about 33 kilos. Not only is this quantity beyond all proportions, it would also have been very expensive.

What would author want to tell us with this formula: *a mixture of myrrh and aloes, about a hundred pounds in weight?* Also in the other gospels we read about balsam that is brought to the grave, but nowhere is specified that it concerns a mixture of two spices.

The total quantity of balsam could be reformulated as: aloes x myrrh = 100.
Converted into numbers would give: 10 x 10 = 100
The number 10 in Greek is *deka*. The first letter of *deka* is a *delta*, written as Δ. In the balm is hidden Δ x Δ, or in other words: the hexagram!

Another curiosity is that embalming the deceased - contrary to what vers 19:30 asserts - was (and is) not at all customary in Judaism. It's even forbidden for Jews to touch dead bodies.
Myrrh was predominantly used in marriage rituals[16]. Esther bathed six months in myrrh before she was brought to king Ahasuerus (also see chapter 3), and in the Song of Solomon, which deals with the sacred marriage, we find many metaphors in which myrrh is mentioned (Song 1:13, 3:6, 4:6, 4:14, 4:16, 5:1, 5:5).
The embalming of Jesus, like the hexagram, is to tell us that the resurrection of Jesus is a result of the sacred marriage that had unfolded (years earlier) within him.

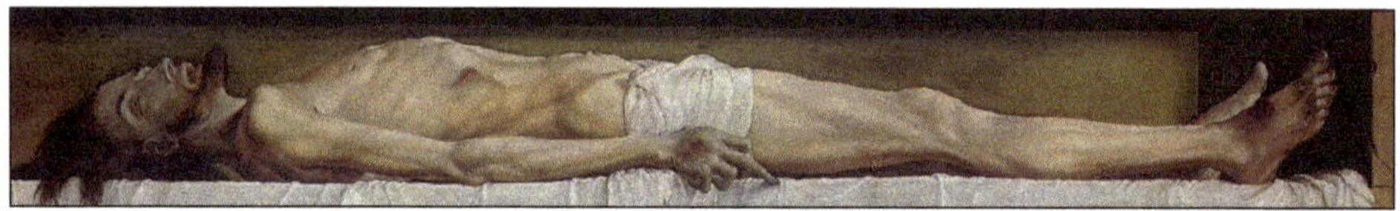

*Hans Holbein the Younger, The Dead Christ in the Tomb, 1521, Kunstmuseum Basel, Switzerland. The extended middle finger of Jesus refers to the "awakened" spinal column: he made of the two one!*

## INRI

The letters INRI appear on virtually every crucifix in the world. This inscription derives from the fourth gospel, in which we read:

*Pilate had a notice prepared and fastened to the cross. It read: "JESUS THE NAZ-ARENE, THE KING OF THE JEWS."*
(John 19:19)

INRI is the acronym of the Latin words Iesus Nazarenus, Rex Iudaeorum. In the other gospels the inscription is shorter. The addition the *Nazarene* is omitted. Most exegetes assume that the *Nazarene* refers to Nazareth, the place where Jesus spent his childhood (Matthew 2:23). But in that time there was no town called Nazareth.

The Greek word *Nazōraios*, which is translated with *Nazarene*, probably derives from the Hebrew *nāzar*, and could be translated with "someone who consecrates."
The Greek *Iesous* ho *Nazōraios* would therefor mean: Jesus the Consecrator. Baptism is a form of consecration. A baptist could be called a *nazōraios*. With this appears a translation of *Iesous* ho *Nazōraios* as: Jesus the Baptist![17]

Nazareth is probably a fictitious city, made up by the evangelists to hide Jesus' epithet Nazarene, and with that to prevent that a connection would be made with John the Baptist. As we saw earlier, the author of the fourth gospel went to great lengths to leave clues as to the true identity of Jesus. The inscription INRI is another example of this.

# Conclusion

The authors of the synoptic gospels write about Mary Magdalene that she was one of the women who followed Jesus and that she was liberated of seven demons. The fourth gospel mentions nothing of this.

In this gospel are no women who follow Jesus, and not a single case of possession.

Inspiring expressions of Jesus that we have thanks to the fourth gospel are:

> *If any one of you is without sin, let him be the first to throw a stone at her.*
> (John 8:7)

> *You will know the truth, and the truth will set you free.*
> (John 8:32)

*Marinus van Reymerswaele, St. Jerome in his Study, 1541, Museo del Prado, Madrid, Spain.*

*On the desk are a crucifix and an opened book, showing an image of the resurrection. Jerome points toward a skull: here both take place.*

*Lucas van Leyden, St. Jerome, ca 1521, Ashmolean Museum, Oxford, UK.*
*Jerome points toward the skull: here the crucifixion takes place.*

*Mateo Cerezo, Magdalena, 1665,
private collection.*

*Mary looks at the crucifix and points toward the
skull: here the crucifixion takes place.*

*Rohan Master, 1435,
illumination from Grandes Heures de Rohan,
Bibliothèque Nationale, Paris, France.*

*The apostle John holds on to Mary, the mother
of Jesus. They depict the merger of the masculine
and the feminine. God points with two fingers
- the sign of the sacred marriage - toward his
head: here all of this takes place.*

*I am the way and the truth and the life. No one comes to the Father except through me.*
(John 14:6)

The most revealing - and least understood - quote from this gospel is possibly:

*I have given them the glory that you gave me, that they may be one as we are one...*
(John 17:22)

The usual interpretation is that the disciples (will) form a unified whole among themselves, just like Jesus formed a unity with God. The "being one" that is meant here, however, is: to be internally no longer divided in a masculine and a feminine half.
Mary Magdalene writes this out of her own experience: Jesus has baptized his disciples with the Holy Spirit: "he gave them the glory," a consecration that leads to a process of rebirth during which the person becomes an only-begotten - a born one, a born into unity - "son or daughter" of God, just like Jesus himself (John 1:14). That the disciples have not (yet) perfected this process, we can deduce from the formulation *"that they may be..."*

In the time of Jesus it would have been no different than nowadays: only a rare individual succeeds in bringing this path to a good end. From what the Bible says about her, we may deduce that Mary Magdalene had achieved a high level of spirituality, still during the lifetime of Jesus.

She was his favorite disciple; the disciple whom he loved the most. The fact that he appeared first to her after his death could be due to her ability to detect his resurrection body: with her sensitivity and receptivity as a consequence of her own awakening.

*He who loves me will be loved by my Father, and I too will love him and show myself to him.*
(John 14:21)

In the next chapter we will examine the bond between Jesus and Mary Magdalene closer. How should we interpret the love that, according to Mary herself, existed between them?

**Christian art**

Remarkably many artists have incorporated in paintings of the crucified Jesus the sign of the sacred marriage. We see Jesus, still alive or already dead, with two extended fingers and/or one extended finger (see examples on pages 136 to 140). The message is in all cases the same: I have made the two into one.

*Jesus said, "When you make the two one, you will become the sons of man*, and when you say, 'Mountain, move away,' it will move away."*
Gospel of Thomas, 106


*    In the Bible, Jesus often refers to himself as the Son of Man. With this he wants to convey that he - as awakened and completed man - personifies a next step in our evolution. A new generation, with a new consciousness: the god-man.

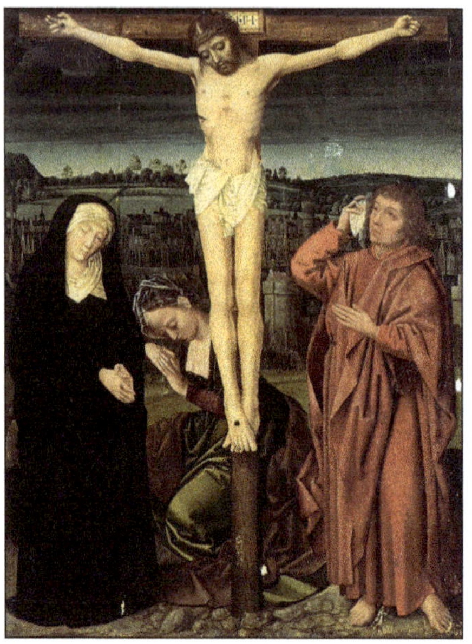

*Adriaen Isenbrandt, early 16th century*

*Anthony van Dyck, 1640*

*English missal for the laity*

*Eric Gill, early 20th century*

*Max Schmalzl, ca 1900*

*Gabriel Wüger, 1868*

*Gerard David, ca 1495*

*Stained glass*

*Stained glass*

*Jacopo Palma il Giovane, 1579*

*Jozef Speybrouck, 1928*

*Josse Lieferinxe, 1500-1505*

Artist and date unknown

Artist unknown, ca 1890

Artist unknown, 16<sup>th</sup> century

Master of the Litoměřice Altarpiece, 1510

*Artist and date unknown*

*Pedro Sánchez de Ezpeleta, 1596*

*Peter Paul Rubens (studio),
early 17th century*

*Roman missal*

# 5

## The animal in man

*We know that anyone born of God does not continue to sin;
the one who was born of God keeps him safe, and the evil one cannot harm him.*

1 John 5:18

The relationship between Jesus and Mary Magdalene is a topic that stirs the imagination: how intimate were they? How probable is it that Jesus even had a relationship with a woman? The Bible says nothing about a wife, but that doesn't mean there was none. But we can, however, read about how Jesus thought about having a sexual relationship. When his disciples ask whether it is better not to marry, he answers:

> *Not everyone can accept this word, but only those to whom it has been given. For some are eunuchs because they were born that way; others were made that way by men; and others have renounced marriage because of the kingdom of heaven. The one who can accept this should accept it.*
> (Matthew 19:11-12)

The word that Jesus uses in this text, eunuchs, describes castrated men whose job it was to guard the wives of the rich and powerful. Jesus does not mean this emasculation literally, but uses it as a metaphor for celibacy, which he recommends to those who want to realize the *Kingdom of Heaven*.

This Kingdom of God was the core of Jesus' preaching. From his words we may deduce that he himself partook in the divine nature, wanted to teach us how we too can achieve this state of consciousness. Throughout the centuries there have been but a few who understood this.

Jesus wrapped many of his lessons in parables, but also the evangelists themselves hid much of what they knew about the divine in metaphors and word-play, intended for the serious seeker for God. Those who enter the symbolic depths of the Bible will begin to understand that Jesus operated on a level of consciousness that was no longer connected with sexual desires. Or as he himself said:

> *The people of this age marry and are given in marriage. But those who are considered worthy of taking part in that age and in the resurrection from the dead will neither marry nor be given in marriage, and they can no longer die; for they are like the angels. They are God's children, since they are children of the resurrection.*
> (Luke 20:34-36)

With "resurrection from the dead," Jesus means a spiritual awakening, and not a physical resurrection of the material body, as many think (1 Cor 15:44). People who are only focused on material things and sensual pleasures, are regarded as "dead" in a spiritual sense. Other descriptions we find in the Bible for the resurrection are: rising, rebirth, deliverance and awakening from sleep.

When the Sadducees critically interrogate Jesus about the topic of resurrection and marriage he answers:

> *You are in error because you do not know the Scriptures or the power of God. At the resurrection people will neither marry nor be given in marriage; they will be like the angels in heaven.*
> (Matthew 22:29-30)

A telling quote. "You don't know the power of God (the kundalini energy)," Jesus says, or else you would understand it. Spiritual awakening is not only becoming aware of the spiritual dimensions of life. It is a complete process of transformation, during which God takes up domicile in the person, who becomes "like an angel."

In this text, Jesus also refers to the Scriptures, to the Old Testament. "You also don't know those…," he says to the Sadducees. This is a bold statement, because they were the religious rulers.

What can we find in the Old Testament about sexuality in relation to spiritual awakening? A great deal, it appears. In virtually every story this topic is discussed. Better yet, one might call it the central theme of the entire Old Testament.
To be able to realize our divine potential we must transform our animal instincts.

When you understand the language of imagery in which the Bible was written, every story appears to contain concrete instructions for spiritual growth. Bloody battles, slavery and animal sacrifices must not be taken literally but depict forces that rage and fight each other, within a person.

We are born with a dual nature. Our lower nature comprises animal drives and derives from the animal origin of our body. In our soul slumbers our higher nature like a divine pilot flame that wants to fan into an blazing fire.

This duality results in a continuous internal tension, whether we realize this or not. The impulses of our animal instincts are often perpendicular to the desires of our soul.

The overwhelming majority of humans lives predominantly according to the lower nature. Qualities such as greed, aggression, lust, jealousy and egoism are animal drives. Whoever opens a newspaper or watches the news on TV sees the animal in humans. Open a random magazine and you will see that we are preoccupied by mostly our appearance (the displaying and grooming of animals), sex and food. Whoever watches sport sees sublimated territorial behavior and rivalry.

And through that chaos of animal drives, the soft voice of our higher nature calls for compassion, servitude, justice and sharing with others.

### Adam and Eve

When Adam and Eve are forced to leave paradise, God dresses them in animals skins (Genesis 3:21). This symbolizes what happens when we incarnate on earth. The person loses contact with his higher nature (paradise, God) and in return receives a body with animal instincts.

The divine serpent withdraws into the pelvis and the person begins life spiritually unconscious. Giving in to the animal instincts keeps the kundalini serpent asleep and so doing the person separated from God.

For a next step in the evolution, from ape-man to god-man, a transformation of the animal drives is required. We require these primal forces, and specifically sexual energy, to realize the divine. The spiritual work consists of the purification and sublimation of these forces (and not their suppression).

The kundalini, or Holy Spirit, is our divine helper on this difficult and long road. When we open ourselves for this transformation process and live a life of purity, God's fire will burn everything that stands between Him and us.

24 So Jacob was left alone, and a man wrestled with him till daybreak.

25 When the man saw that he could not overpower him, he touched the socket of Jacob's hip so that his hip was wrenched as he wrestled with the man.

26 Then the man said, "Let me go, for it is daybreak." But Jacob replied, "I will not let you go unless you bless me."

27 The man asked him, "What is your name?" "Jacob," he answered.

28 Then the man said, "Your name will no longer be Jacob, but Israel, because you have struggled with God and with humans and have overcome."

29 Jacob said, "Please tell me your name." But he replied, "Why do you ask my name?" Then he blessed him there.

30 So Jacob called the place Peniel, saying, "It is because I saw God face to face, and yet my life was spared."

31 The sun rose above him as he passed Peniel, and he was limping because of his hip.

32 Therefore to this day the Israelites do not eat the tendon attached to the socket of the hip, because the socket of Jacob's hip was touched near the tendon.

(Genesis 32:24-32)

*Blessed is the man who perseveres under trial, because when he has stood the test,
he will receive the crown of life...*
(James 1:12)

# Jacob and the angel

The story of the patriarch Jacob, who wrestled with an angel and so doing sustained an injury to his hip, is a beautiful example of the symbolism in the Bible related to obtaining mastery over sexual drives.

After Jacob has transported his family and all his possession across a river (a metaphor for transformation), he gets into a mysterious fight with an unknown man (verse 24).

In Hosea 12:3-4 we read that Jacob's mysterious antagonist was an angel:
*...as a man he struggled with God.*
*He struggled with the angel and overcame him;*
*he wept and begged for his favor.*

This curious fight, full of strange details, is a metaphor for Jacob's wrestling with himself, or better yet: with his sex drive. He overcomes, but he is left with a limp from the fight (verse 31). The dislocation of his hip joint is a euphemism for the deactivation of his genitalia. The Hebrew word *yarek* that is translated with hip also means genitalia.

The name Peniel, which Jacob gives to the place where the fight has taken place (verse 30), refers to the pineal gland, the *glandula pinealis* in Latin; the gland that upon activation brings about a divine experience. The confirmation of this interpretation we receive from Jacob himself. He calls the place Peniel, because he *saw God face to face.*

Jacob wrestled with his sex drive and overcame it. The angel (the kundalini energy) deactivated his sex drive and activated the pineal gland. Jacob achieved eternal life with God (his *life is spared*; verse 30). The *sun rose above him* (verse 31): he is enlightened.

He receives from the angel a new name: *Israel*, a name that made history. Jacob's numerous descendants even began to call themselves Israelites. The name Israel became a badge of honor, because this people would have been chosen by God.

However, when we look at the meaning of the name Israel, a new light comes to shine upon this "being chosen." The ancient Hebrew alphabet consisted of pictograms. Letters were not abstract symbols but little drawings with names and meanings. Words that were formed from these pictograms resembled cartoons of which every character had a separate meaning.

The authors of the Old Testament made lavish use of the symbolic meaning of the letters, to either hide messages or make them clear.[18]

The name Israel in Hebrew is: לארשי

To the Jews, the second letter, the *shin*, is connected with God. When we review the original pictogram, it becomes clear why. The *shin* consists of a horizontal line with three vertical lines: a depiction of the three energy channels that are involved with a kundalini awakening!

Then follows the letter "*resh*"; a word that also means "head." The ancient Hebrew pictogram for this letter is therefore the head of a man: ৭

*El*, the final syllable, means God.

Finally, the first letter, the *yod*, of which the meaning depends on the rest of a word, may here be translated as "he does."

The name Israel, which Jacob receives from the angel, appears to be a cartoon story of what happened that night: he has brought the kundalini-energy (*shin*) to the head (*resh*) and has seen God (*El*) face to face. He has spiritually awakened.

To understand the Bible, this meaning is of immense importance. In the Bible, "an Israelite" is someone who has realized his higher nature; someone who is circumcised in the spiritual sense.
The apostle Paul confirms this in his letter to the Romans:

> *…not all who are descended from Israel are Israel.*
> (Romans 9:6)

> *A man is not a Jew if he is only one outwardly, nor is circumcision merely outward and physical. No, a man is a Jew if he is one inwardly; and circumcision is circumcision of the heart, by the Spirit, not by the written code. Such a man's praise is not from men, but from God.*
> (Romans 2:28-29)

All the wars and other precarious circumstances that befall the Israelites in the Old Testament are metaphors for the universal battle in the man between his higher nature (symbolized by the Israelites) and his lower nature (the opponents).
The "chosen ones" are all those who are found worthy by God to enter the Promised Land (paradise, the Kingdom of God); all who are spiritually circumcised.

## Moses

Also the genitalia of Moses get dealt with. He and his wife Zipporah are on their way to Egypt, when in an inn, God wants to kill his loyal prophet. A reason is not given:

*24 At a lodging place on the way, the Lord met Moses and was about to kill him.*
*25 But Zipporah took a flint knife, cut off her son's foreskin and touched Moses' feet*
*with it. "Surely you are a bridegroom of blood to me," she said.*
*26 So the Lord let him alone. (At that time she said "bridegroom of blood," refer-*
*ring to circumcision.)*
(Exodus 4:24-26)

This story too we are not to take literally. Circumcision symbolizes the curbing of the sexual drives. Zipporah takes the foreskin of her son and makes it touch the feet of Moses (verse 25). From this we me derive that the "circumcision" is actually about Moses himself. A son or daughter in the Bible often represents the "new man."

What God wanted to kill was the "old man" Moses, who lived out of his lower nature. Zipporah, as personification of the feminine aspect of God, of the kundalini, performs the "circumcision." The flint knife she uses refers to the kundalini fire.

After this, Zipporah calls Moses *bridegroom of blood* (verse 26). This emphasizes that the whole scene is about an inner spiritual process. Moses and Zipporah represent the inner masculine and feminine. They have "the same blood."

# The fall of Jericho

The story of the fall of the city of Jericho, under the leadership of Joshua, also contains rich and beautiful symbolism. Surprisingly, a prostitute plays a heroic part.

After a journey of forty years through the desert, Joshua, the successor of Moses, and his people have arrived at the first city of the promised land Canaan: Jericho.

*1 Now Jericho was tightly shut up because of the Israelites. No one went out and*
*no one came in.*
*2 Then the Lord said to Joshua, "See, I have delivered Jericho into your hands,*
*along with its king and its fighting men.*

*3 March around the city once with all the armed men. Do this for six days.*
*4 Have seven priests carry trumpets of rams' horns in front of the ark. On the seventh day, march around the city seven times, with the priests blowing the trumpets.*
*5 When you hear them sound a long blast on the trumpets, have all the people give a loud shout; then the wall of the city will collapse and the people will go up, every man straight in "*
(Joshua 6:1-5)

Joshua follows God's instructions and on the seventh day the walls of Jericho collapse and Jericho is invaded.

*24 Then they burned the whole city and everything in it, but they put the silver and gold and the articles of bronze and iron into the treasury of the Lord 's house.*
*25 But Joshua spared Rahab the prostitute, with her family and all who belonged to her, because she hid the men Joshua had sent as spies to Jericho-and she lives among the Israelites to this day.*
(Joshua 6:24-25)

An important aspect of the Jewish prayer ritual is the strapping on of the *tefillin*. These are two leather straps with attached to them a little black box that contains fragments from the Torah.
One prayer strap is wound seven times around the arm, with the box on the biceps, at the level of the heart.
The other is tied to the head in such a way that the box is positioned on the front of the head, with the two ends of the strap hanging forward, left and right of the neck. On the black boxes appears the letter *shin*, the first letter of the name of God: *Shaddai*.

We recognize in the winding of the strap around the arm the spiral movement of the kundalini - Shekinah in Jewish mysticism - through the seven chakras.
The box on the front of the head (according to the Torah, actually "between the eyes") marks the pineal gland:

*Therefore shall ye lay up these my words in your heart and in your soul, and bind them for a sign upon your hand, that they may be as frontlets between your eyes.*
(Deuteronomy 11:18, KJ21)

Source: www.wikihow.com

The two ends of the prayer strap left and right by the neck depict the two energy channels that flow along the spinal column and during a kundalini awakening merge at the center of the head.

The letter *shin*, written as a "trident," refers to the divine energy that opens the heart chakra and activates the pineal gland (the two locations where the black boxes are placed).

### The deeper meaning of this story

*Jericho means city of the moon.* The moon symbolizes matter, that must be conquered (also see chapter 2).

*The ark of the covenant* (verse 4) symbolizes the divine.

On certain Jewish holidays, the ram's horn, the shofar, is still sounded.

The circular trajectory that the priests and the ark are to follow around the city (verses 3 and 4), depicts the spiral movement of the kundalini energy.

The sounding of the rams' horns (verse 4)- i.e. blowing air in spiral shaped horns - symbolizes the kundalini that rises through the spinal column.

The number seven (the number of days, priests, rams' horns, circles around the city) refers to the seven chakras.

The *fire* with which the city is burned (verse 24) depicts the divine fire that burns everything that stand between man and God. Only that which belongs to our higher nature (the treasury) is preserved.

## Rachab

The *prostitute Rahab* (verse 25) symbolizes the kundalini that manifests itself in the pelvis as sexual energy. In this story, this energy is sublimated (brought to the crown). This we can deduce from the location of Rahab's house, which is located at great height: *for her house was upon the town wall, and she dwelt upon the wall* (Joshua 2:15 KJ21).

Guided upward, the sexual forces become the vehicle for the divine.



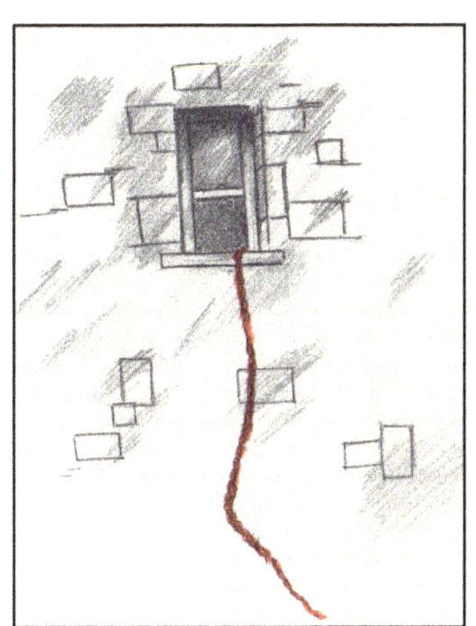

Rahab helps the spies of Joshua escape the city by means of a scarlet cord that she hangs from her window. This orange-red cord, which symbolizes the kundalini fire, also becomes her own salvation when Jericho falls: *Behold, when we come into the land, thou shalt bind this line of scarlet thread in the window which thou didst let us down by* (Joshua 2:18).
Joshua's men murder all inhabitants of Jericho but through the cord Rahab is saved.

In multiple spiritual traditions (among others Buddhism, Hinduism and Kabbalah), a red cord is worn - whether or not around the wrist - as amulet for matters like protection, fertility, healing and happiness. All aspects of a kundalini awakening.
In the Kabbalistic tradition, the red wrist band, in order to work, has to come from a cord that was wound seven times (the kundalini movement up through the chakras) around the grave of matriarch Rachel.

From her name too we can deduce that Rahab symbolizes the kundalini. Rahab is a contraction of the Hebrew *ruah* (spirit) and *ab* (father): the Spirit of the Father, or the Spirit of God.

That we mustn't take the story of the fall of Jericho literally, is also demonstrated by what we read about Rahab in the final sentence: *she lives among* [Hebrew: *beqereb*; **in the middle of**] *the Israelites to this day* (verse 25). The Spirit of God flows to this day through the spinal column ("in the middle") of the awakened person (Israel).

**Visual Art**

In many Christian Renaissance paintings we see the infant Jesus wearing a necklace or bracelet made of red coral. In that time, people believed red coral provided protection against witchcraft, disease and bad fortune. From the other symbolism in those same paintings we can deduce that the painters used the red coral as esoteric symbol for a kundalini awakening.

**The moral of this story:** to realize the divine (the captured treasures of Jericho), the sexual energy must be sublimated.

a.  Ambrogio Borgognone, ca 1500
    The infant Jesus holds a string of red coral in his hand, and with his other hand he makes the sign
    of the sacred marriage: "I made the two one." In his aureole we see the fleur-de-lis, a symbol
    for the pineal gland (see appendix 1).

b.

c.

b.  Unknown artist, Tuscan School, late 15$^{th}$ century.
    The infant Jesus wears a necklace and bracelet of red coral. He holds on to the translucent shawl of his mother. The shawl winds like a serpent, upward to the head of Mary and terminates in a knob (the pineal gland).

c.  Angelo Puccinelli
    The infant Jesus wears a necklace with a red coral pendant. The two fingers of Mary, with the piece of red coral between them, symbolize the three energy channels that are involved in a kundalini awakening.

# Susanna and the elders

In Catholic and Orthodox Bibles we find in the Book of Daniel the story of the beautiful Susanna, who is accosted by two elders while bathing (this story is not incorporated in Protestant Bibles).

Susanna too represents the kundalini, or Holy Spirit, in the pelvis. A water source is one of the universal metaphors for this energy. The Greek name Susanna is a transliteration of the Hebrew word *shushan*, *shoshan* or *shoshannah*, which means lily. To the Egyptians and the Jews the lily has the same meaning as the lotus does to the eastern traditions: both flowers represent purity and spiritual perfection.

Etymologically too there appears to be a connection. The energy channel in the spinal column through which the kundalini flows upward to the head, is called *sushumna* in eastern traditions. This is a word that resembles the name Susanna (*shoshannah*).

Susanna is married to Joiakim, whose name means "God raises up." Joiakim and Susanna together form the image of the kundalini that is "raised up".

## *Dishonorable proposals in a closed off garden*

On a certain day, Susanna takes a bath in a closed off section of the garden. This image evokes associations with the Song of Solomon, in which the serenaded beloved is also situated in a closed off garden: *You are a garden locked up, my sister, my bride; you are a spring enclosed, a sealed fountain* (Song of Solomon 4:12).

15 Once, while they were watching for an opportune day, she went in as before with only two maids, and wished to bathe in the garden, for it was very hot. 16 And no one was there except the two elders, who had hid themselves and were watching her. 17 She said to her maids, "Bring me oil and ointments, and shut the garden doors so that I may bathe." 18 They did as she said, shut the garden doors, and went out by the side doors to bring what they had been commanded; and they did not see the elders, because they were hidden. 19 When the maids had gone out, the two elders rose and ran to her, and said: 20 "Look, the garden doors are shut, no one sees us, and we are in love with you; so give your consent, and lie with us. 21 If you refuse, we will testify against you that a young man was with you, and this was why you sent your maids away." 22 Susanna sighed deeply, and said, "I am hemmed in on every side. For if I do this thing, it is death for me; and if I do not, I shall not escape your hands. 23 I choose not to do it and to fall into your hands, rather than to sin in the sight of the Lord." 24 Then Susanna cried out with a loud voice, and the two elders shouted against her. 25 And one of them ran and opened the garden doors. 26 When the household servants heard the shouting in the garden, they rushed in at the side door to see what had happened to her. 27 And when the elders told their tale, the servants were greatly ashamed, for nothing like this had ever been said about Susanna.
(Daniel 13:15-27 Revised Standard Version Catholic Edition)


54 Now then, if you really saw her, tell me this: Under what tree did you see them being intimate with each other?" He answered, "Under a mastic tree." 55 And Daniel said, "Very well! You have lied against your own head, for the angel of God has received the sentence from God and will immediately cut you in two." 56 Then he put him aside, and commanded them to bring the other. And he said to him, "You offspring of Canaan and not of Judah, beauty has deceived you and lust has perverted your heart. 57 This is how you both have been dealing with the daughters of Israel, and they were intimate with you through fear; but a daughter of Judah would not endure your wickedness. 58 Now then, tell me: Under what tree did you catch them being intimate with each other?" He answered, "Under an evergreen oak." 59 And Daniel said to him, "Very well! You also have lied against your own head, for the angel of God is waiting with his sword to saw you in two, that he may destroy you both." 60 Then all the assembly shouted loudly and blessed God, who saves those who hope in him. 61 And they rose against the two elders, for out of their own mouths Daniel had convicted them of bearing false witness; 62 and they did to them as they had wickedly planned to do to their neighbor; acting in accordance with the law of Moses, they put them to death. Thus innocent blood was saved that day.
(Daniel 13:54-62 Revised Standard Version Catholic Edition)

As we saw in chapter 3, this beloved represents the divine energy in the pelvis (the closed off garden).

Two elders, acquaintances of her husband, spy on Susanna as she bathes. When the maids have left, they emerge and blackmail Susanna: if she doesn't have intercourse with them, they will report her for adultery with another man (verses 20-21) - a charge which in that time would have resulted in stoning. Because Susanna does not yield to their dishonorable proposal, they execute their threat and Susanna is condemned to death.

In the nick of time, Daniel, after whom the Bible Book is named, comes into play. He separates the men and asks both under which tree the supposed adultery would have been committed. The men give different answers, which proves the innocence of Susanna (verses 54-59). A tree is a classic metaphor for the awakened kundalini energy.

### The moral

Susanna refuses to have intercourse with the lustful men. This ends well for her; her assailers are killed.
The two elders represent the two energy channels that connect us with duality. This is confirmed by Daniel in the text: *the angel of God has received the sentence from God and will immediately cut you in two* (verses 55 and 59).
When the kundalini energy is not deployed to gratify feelings of lust, but is "raised up" (Joiakim), the duality in a person (the two elders) will cease to exist.

## David and Bathsheba

From the story about king David and Bathsheba we can learn what happens when we do give in the feelings of lust (2 Samuel 11). David also sees a beautiful woman bathing:

> *One evening David got up from his bed and walked around on the roof of the palace. From the roof he saw a woman bathing. The woman was very beautiful.* (2 Samuel 11:2)

*Michiel Coxie, Susanna and the Elders, 1560.*

*A robe of fur is draped around Susanna; a reference to the animalistic behavior of the two men by which she is surrounded. The two hands of the men are depicted in such a way that they evoke associations with vertebrae; a reference to the spinal column through which the kundalini (Susanna) flows.*

Bathsheba is the wife of Uriah, one of the army commanders of David. This, however, does not keep him from having her brought to him by his messengers and "sleep" with her (2 Samuel 11:4), after which she appears pregnant. David subsequently concocts a plan because of which Uriah is killed in battle.

The name Bathsheba means "daughter of seven", a reference to the kundalini energy that flows through the seven chakras. This name strongly reminds of the queen of Sheba (seven), who has a special encounter with David's son and successor king Solomon. As we saw in chapter 3, she too stands for the divine energy in our pelvis. The name Uriah means "flame of the Lord."

David sees Bathsheba from the roof of his house. This depicts his spiritual level: de kundalini energy flows through his entire spinal column, up to the crown chakra (the roof). He forfeits this, however, by surrendering to lust and adultery: he kills Uriah - the flame of God.

In the quote above we read that it was evening and that David *got up from his bed*; two metaphors that are supposed to tell us about his spiritual situation. His consciousness was unenlightened (evening) and he was asleep (was spiritually unaware).

The repercussions are dire. God does not approve this behavior and kills the son that is born from this union. The meaning of this is: when the awakened kundalini energy (David on the roof) is used for sexuality, it leads to (spiritual) death.


## Power over the flesh

The stories of the Old Testament are clear: it is God or the underbelly. Jesus concurs with this in his sermon about the coming of the Kingdom of God, in the gospel of Luke:

He draws a few interesting parallels:
- *just as it happened in the days of Noah…* (verse 26)
- *It was the same as happened in the days of Lot…* (verse 28)
- *Remember Lot's wife* (verse 32)

20 Now He was questioned by the Pharisees as to when the kingdom of God was coming, and He answered them and said, "The kingdom of God is not coming with signs that can be observed;

21 nor will they say, 'Look, here it is!' or, 'There it is!' For behold, the kingdom of God is in your midst."

22 And He said to the disciples, "The days will come when you will long to see one of the days of the Son of Man, and you will not see it.

23 And they will say to you, 'Look there,' or, 'Look here!' Do not leave, and do not run after them.

24 For just like the lightning, when it flashes out of one part of the sky, shines to the other part of the sky, so will the Son of Man be in His day.

25 But first He must suffer many things and be rejected by this generation.

26 And just as it happened in the days of Noah, so will it also be in the days of the Son of Man:

27 people were eating, they were drinking, they were marrying, and they were being given in marriage, until the day that Noah entered the ark, and the flood came and destroyed them all.

28 It was the same as happened in the days of Lot: they were eating, they were drinking, they were buying, they were selling, they were planting, and they were building;

29 but on the day that Lot left Sodom, it rained fire and brimstone from heaven and destroyed them all.

30 It will be just the same on the day that the Son of Man is revealed.

31 On that day, the one who will be on the housetop, with his goods in the house, must not go down to take them out; and likewise the one in the field must not turn back.

32 Remember Lot's wife.

33 Whoever strives to save his life will lose it, and whoever loses his life will keep it.

34 I tell you, on that night there will be two in one bed; one will be taken and the other will be left.

35 There will be two women grinding at the same place; one will be taken and the other will be left.

36 Two men will be in the field; one will be taken and the other will be left."

37 And responding, they *said to Him, "Where, Lord?" And He said to them, "Where the body is, there also the vultures will be gathered."

(Luke 17:20-37, NAS)

And he makes a few pithy, clarifying statements:
- *the kingdom of God is in your midst"* (verse 21)
- *Whoever strives to save his life will lose it, and whoever loses his life will keep it* (verse 33)
- *Where the body is, there also the vultures will be gathered* (verse 37)

Jesus starts in verse 21 with a statement that should be printed on the cover of the New Testament: *the kingdom of God is in your midst* After that he tells his disciples what his return to earth will look like (read: what happens when God takes up domicile within us).

The images of death and disaster from the stories of Noah and Lot which follow, symbolize the first phase in the process that leads to the unification with God: an inner purification by the kundalini, or Holy Spirit.
The flood from the story of Noah (verses 26-27) is a metaphor for the cleansing of a person.

The first thing Noah does when he has solid ground under his feet again is bring an animal sacrifice (Genesis 8:20). The deeper meaning of this is that our animal nature must be "sacrificed" to be able to experience the divine.

**In paintings**
Michelangelo effectively incorporated this deeper meaning of Noah's sacrifice in his famous Sistine Chapel frescoes. Depicted are two of Noah's sons, both naked, with the sacrificial animals clasped between their legs. This image is supposed to tell us that the sheep that are being sacrificed represent the sexual drives. In agreement with the rest of the symbolism, the sacrificial fire burns at the level of Noah's underbelly (page 164).

Also the story of Lot is about inner purification (Genesis 19). In this case a (kundalini) fire totally burns down the cities from which Lot departs - Sodom and Gomorrah. These cities, where godlessness dominates, represent the lower nature, which Lot "leaves behind".

*Michelangelo, Sacrifice of Noah, 1508-1512, Sistine Chapel, Rome*

Jesus emphatically advises his disciples to not turn back, or retrieve goods from their houses, when these signs appear (verse 31). God purifies us, but it is up to us to detach and let go of the past. If we don't the process of awakening comes to a halt.

*Zoutpilaren*

*Remember Lot's wife*, says Jesus (verse 32). The wife of Lot did look back during the flight from Sodom and Gomorrah and she turned into a pillar of salt - a beautiful metaphor for the inner world of a person who is "stuck" in his past: in ingrained patterns, old pain and false convictions. The ego is, in a manner of speaking, "crystalized." It is motionless and lifeless.

164

Whoever wants to inherit eternal life in the Kingdom of God will have to let go of his old life and the old man (verse 33).

Jesus concludes his sermon with a beautiful one-liner that pithily summarizes his teachings: *Where the body is, there also the vultures will be gathered* (verse 37). Being focused on the body and the animal drives attached to it, brings about "death" in a spiritual sense.

The apostle Paul says it like this:

> *But if the Spirit of Him who raised Jesus from the dead dwells in you, He who raised Christ Jesus from the dead will also give life to your mortal bodies through His Spirit who dwells in you. So then, brothers and sisters, we are under obligation, not to the flesh, to live according to the flesh — for if you are living in accord with the flesh, you are going to die; but if by the Spirit you are putting to death the deeds of the body, you will live.*
> (Romans 8:11-13 NAS)

In the gospel of Thomas Jesus commends virginity:

> *A woman from the crowd said to him, "Blessed are the womb which bore you and the breasts which nourished you."*
> *He said to her, "Blessed are those who have heard the word of the father and have truly kept it. For there will be days when you will say, 'Blessed are the womb which has not conceived and the breasts which have not given milk.'"*
> Gospel of Thomas:79

## But...

Aren't we allowed to enjoy anything, then? We most certainly are! The key-word is detachment; not being attached to certain experiences, not striving for sensual pleasures. Being awakened means being free. The awakened person experiences bliss without the need for sensual stimulation.

These teachings of Jesus, incidentally, are not new. What he said does not essentially differ from what, for example, the Buddha said.
His message of detachment ("conquering the world") is universal and timeless.

*Francesco Squarcione, 15th century,
Musei Civici of Padua, Italy.*

*To the right we see John the Baptist, with his
"loins girded" and his hand at the level of his
crotch; a reference to mastery over the sexual
drives.*

*William Blake, illustration of John Milton's
Paradise Lost, 1808,
National Gallery of Victoria,
Melbourne, Australia.*

*Satan observes Adam and Eve being intimate-
ly together. This image forges an association
between the physical intimacy of Adam and
Eve and the "paradise lost": by allowing energy to flow off via the underbelly (sexual activ-
ity), the person loses contact with the divine.*

Lambert Hopfer, Adam and Eve,
16*th* century, Detroit Institute of Arts, USA.

Josse Lieferinxe,
St. Michael killing the Dragon, *circa 1490*,
*Musée du Petit Palais, Avignon, France.*

*Eve accepts a forbidden fruit from the serpent. Adam's hand lies on Eve's breast. The image suggests a connection between sexuality and eating the forbidden fruits.*

*The battle between Saint Michael and the dragon (from the Book of Revelation) is a metaphor for man's inner battle between his higher, divine nature and his animalistic sexual desires. The leg of the dragon in the crotch of the archangel is a reference to this deeper meaning.*

*Moretto da Brescia, St Justina with the Unicorn, circa 1530,*
*Kunsthistorisches Museum, Vienna, Austria.*

Also in Christian iconography we find the unicorn. Mary, the mother of Jesus, is sometimes depicted with a unicorn in a closed off garden (both referring to her virginity). Above, we see saint Justina depicted with a unicorn. In the fabric of the garment of the saint we see, next to the horn, a pinecone pattern; a reference to the pineal gland.

Don't worry!
The celibate, awakened person is all but a "dry tree"!

*let not any eunuch complain, "I am only a dry tree."*
*For this is what the Lord says:*
*"To the eunuchs who keep my Sabbaths,*
*who choose what pleases me and hold fast to my covenant,*
*to them I will give within my temple and its walls a memorial and a name*
*better than sons and daughters;*
*I will give them an everlasting name*
*that will not be cut off.*
(Isaiah 56:3-5)

**The unicorn**
A universal symbol of sublimated animal energy is the unicorn.
His white color symbolizes that the animalistic forces have been purified. The spiraling horn on the forehead of the animal, the place where the sacred marriage takes place, refers to the sublimation of the kundalini energy.

According to the legends, a unicorn can only be captured by placing a virgin under a tree. He will let himself be lured by the virgin and will then fall asleep on her lap. The tree represents the awakened kundalini energy. The sexual energy must be preserved (the virgin) for the spiritual process of awakening. The animal drives in the belly (the lap) of a person must "fall asleep."

The legends also say that he horn of the animal can purify poisoned water and cure diseases. Purification and healing are both aspects of the kundalini. The unicorn would also be able to track down hidden water sources (the kundalini).

# Conclusion

To return to the question with which we started this chapter: did Mary Magdalena and Jesus have a sexual relationship? This is highly improbable, judging from Jesus' own words and the Scriptures.

Mary has Jesus say:
*I have overcome the world* (John 16:33).

And also:
These words spoke Jesus and lifted up His eyes to Heaven and said, "Father, the hour is come. Glorify Thy Son, that Thy Son also may glorify Thee, **as Thou hast given Him power over all flesh**, that He should give eternal life to as many as Thou hast given Him.
(John 17:1-2 KJ21)

This reveals that the body and matter no longer had a grip on him.
When Mary writes about herself as "the disciple whom Jesus loved," she uses the Greek *agape*, love without eros.

Mary reclined on Jesus' bosom (John 13:23). Their intimate connection was at the level of the heart. They both had experienced a spiritual process of inner "resurrection" and were like the "angels of God" who don't marry (Matthew 22:30).

In her gospel, Mary uses her own character and that of Jesus to depict the inner merger of the masculine and feminine - the sacred marriage. At the level of the archetypes, Jesus and Mary Magdalene represent forces in us that want to unite. In us the voice of Jesus sounds as he calls: *Mary!* In us Mary responds: *Rabboni!* They yearn to embrace each other.

And God already extends His hand to us.

> *I will betroth you to me forever;*
> *I will betroth you in righteousness and justice,*
> *in love and compassion.*
> *I will betroth you in faithfulness,*
> *and you will acknowledge the Lord.*
> (Hosea 2:18-19)

Eric Gill, Nuptials of God, 1922,
National Galleries of Scotland, Edinburgh.

## Archbasilica of Saint John Lateran

The statues on the roof of the Archbasilica of Saint John Lateran, in the heart of Rome, reflect, in the sight of the whole world, all main themes that have been discussed in this book.

John the Baptist, to the left of Jesus, holds a cross in his hand instead of his more common iconographic attribute: a banner that says Ecce Agnus Dei (See the Lamb of God). The cross is an attribute of Jesus. With this "swap of attributes", that can also be found in many paintings and which for centuries nobody seems to have noticed, the artist wants to let us know that John the Baptist was Jesus.

The evangelist John, to the right of Jesus, with a bare shoulder, resembles a woman: the author of the fourth gospel was not John but Mary Magdalene.

Jesus protrudes two extended fingers forward: he has made of the two one.

*Also in the interior of the cathedral we find these themes. On the Sacred Door of the basilica, for instance, Mary, the mother of Jesus, points with two fingers up to her crucified son.*

# Notes

1.  See for an extensive analysis of the story of the Tower of Babel my book *Kundalini Awakening in the Bible*.

2.  The word evangel comes from the Greek *euaggelion* and means good (or glad) message.

3.  See for extensive argumentation and analysis of the seven chakras in the gospel of John my book *Kundalini Awakening in the Bible*.

4.  See for an extensive analysis of the story of Raising Lazarus my book *Kundalini Awakening in the Bible*.

5.  See for a discussion of the Egyptian myth of Osiris and the ritual of Raising the Djed my book *Kundalini Awakening in the Bible*.

6.  See for a discussion of the transformation of Abram to Abraham, and the deeper meaning of the Hebrew letter he, my book *Kundalini Awakening in the Bible*.

7.  See for a discussion of the twelve energy channels of the heart chakra in the Bible my book *Kundalini Awakening in the Bible*.

8.  Quote from my book *Kundalini Awakening in the Bible*.

9.  See for a discussion of the symbolism in the Bible my book *Ecce Homo*.

10. See for an extensive analysis of the story of the building of the temple of Solomon my book *Kundalini Awakening in the Bible*.

11. *John the Baptist who became Jesus the Christ*, ISBN 978-90-825023-1-2.

12. See my book *John the Baptist who became Jesus the Christ*.

13. See for a discussion of, and the meaning of, the decapitation of John the Baptist my book *John the Baptist who became Jesus the Christ*.

14. See for the deeper meaning of the crucifixion and resurrection of Jesus my book *Ecce Homo*.

15. See for an extensive analysis of the Genesis story of Adam and Eve my book *Kundalini Awakening in the Bible*.

16. Source: www.abarim-publications.com, pages '*Myrrh, the oil of joy and weddings nights*' and 'Nicodemus and the myrrh oil'

17. See for a more extensive discussion of the name Jesus of Nazareth my book *John the Baptist who became Jesus the Christ*.

18. See for many examples my book *Kundalini Awakening in the Bible*.

19. See for an extensive analysis of the story of the flood my book *Kundalini Awakening in the Bible*.


## Bible quotes:

Unless marked otherwise, the Bible quotes in this book are from the New International Version (NIV).

# Appendix 1 - Symbolism in the Catholic Church

Also in the Christian church we find references to the universal process of God-realization, that begins with the awakening of the divine energy source (the kundalini) in our pelvis.

We already saw in chapter 3 that the anointment of priests and confirmands (confirmation is one of the seven sacraments of the Catholic church) is an external ritual that refers to the change in brain fluid due to the activation of the pineal gland.

**Other examples are:**
1. The cross of ashes on Ash Wednesday
2. The mitre and crosier of high-ranking clergy
3. The lily
4. The fleur-de-lis
5. Chi-Rho
6. IHS
7. The anchor

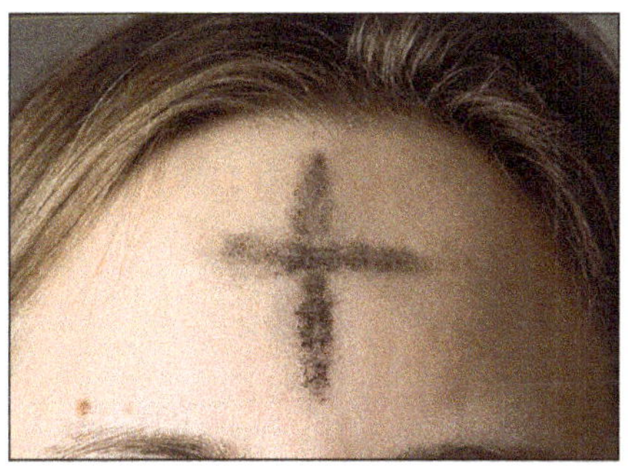

### 1. *The cross of ashes*
Annually, at the beginning of Lent, on Ash Wednesday, believers receive a cross of ashes on their forehead from the priest. He pronounces the dictum: "Remember that you are dust, and to dust you shall return."
Like an anointing, this ritual too refers to an internal process. When the awakened kundalini energy has arrived at the forehead, the ego "dies." The "old man" is discarded, to make way for God.

## 2. Mitre and crosier

The mitre, which bishops, cardinals and the pope wear, has the shape of a pine cone, which refers to the pineal gland. The two ribbons ("*infulae*") at the back of the mitre depict the two energy channels that merge at the level of the forehead (the pineal gland), upon the process of awakening.

The crosier of high ranking clergy - an external symbol of authority - represents, parallel to the esoteric meaning of a staff in the Bible (for instance the staff of Moses), the spinal column with in it the awakened kundalini. The crosier commonly comes with attributes that refer to the process of spiritual awakening: a serpent, a bird, an angel or a pine cone, for example.

a.

b.

a. A staff from the Eastern Orthodox church, with two serpents that bend toward the cross.
b. A 12th century bishop's staff (Diocesan Museum Bamberg) with serpent, which bends toward the pineal gland, and as extra attribute the annunciation (the announcement of the birth of Jesus to Mary), with the angel pointing toward a pillar (see chapter 2 for the pillar as symbol of the spinal column).

c.

d.

c.  *Giovanni Battista Giovenone, The Mystic Marriage of Saint Catherine, 1547, Museo Borgogna, Vercelli, Italy.*
    *The infant Jesus puts a ring on the finger of Saint Catherine, as a sign of their mystic marriage. The deliberately placed crosier declares that the mystic marriage is a consequence of a kundalini awakening in the spinal column of Saint Catherine. The right hand of the bishop makes the sign of the sacred marriage (two fingers together: 2=1).*
d.  *Muster G.Z., 1420-1430, Metropolitan Museum of Art, New York, USA.*
    *The infant Jesus makes the sign of the sacred marriage while holding on to the crosier of the bishop.*

e.    Parmigianino, (attr.), early 16th century, Metropolitan Museum of Art, New York, USA.
f.    Francesco di Giorgio Martini, circa 1490, Museo Thyssen-Bornemisza, Madrid, Spain.
g. J acomart (detail of a diptych), circa 1450, Museo de Bellas Artes, Valencia, Spain.

### 3. *The lily*

As we saw in chapter 5, in ancient Egypt and Judaism the lily refers to purity and a completed process of spiritual awakening, comparable with the lotus flower in eastern traditions. At the energetic level, the lily represents an opened crown chakra.

Also in Christianity the lily is a familiar symbol and has received the official meaning of *virginity*. Saints are sometimes depicted with a lily and the angel Gabriel often has a lily in his hand when he announces the birth of Jesus to Mary - the so-called *annunciation*.

The Bible story of the virgin conception of the Christ Child represents an event that takes place within the soul of a person: the final result of a process of kundalini awakening. Maria personifies in this story the soul of the person who "gives birth" to the divine.

Artists who were aware of this deeper meaning of the conception and birth of Christ have used in paintings of the annunciation (among others) the lily to refer to the spinal column, and with this the process of kundalini awakening.

We see, for instance, solitary lilies on ostensibly long stems and only at the top flowers. Or the lily is positioned to extend the spinal column of Mary of Jesus (images e. and f.). Or the stem with leaves strongly resembles a spinal column (images g. to k.).

h.

i.

j.

k.

h.  Cosimo Rosselli (detail), 1473, Musée du Petit Palais, Avignon, France.
i.  Dante Gabriel Rossetti, circa 1849, Tate Britain, London, UK.
j.  Taddeo Gaddi, circa 1345, Museum Bandini, Fiesole, Italy.
k.  Niccolò di Pietro Gerini, circa 1390, church of Santa Felicita, Florence, Italy.

### 4. The fleur-de-lis

Symbolically speaking, the lily is closely related to the fleur-de-lis, which indeed somewhat resembles a stylized lily. The fleur-de-lis is a symbol that we can find globally in spiritual traditions, and that on a deeper level refers to the pineal gland (the central "petal"). The two outer "petals" of the fleur-de-lis symbolize the two energy channels that merge in the head when the sacred marriage takes place.

Christianity too has embraced the fleur-de-lis. We see it often on, among others, vestment (liturgic garments), crosiers, crockery, crowns of saints, and in the interior of churches (ornaments and paintings). The fleur-de-lis is also sometimes added to the aureole of Jesus. From the rest of the symbolism in a painting we can deduce whether the artist wants to refer to a kundalini awakening with the fleur-de-lis (see images l.).

*l. Fleur-de-lis in the aureole of the Christ Child.*

*Master of the Housebook, Passion altar, 1470, Augustinian Museum, Freiburg, Germany.*

*Albrecht Dürer, Circumcision of Jezus, circa 1497,*
*Gemäldegalerie Alte Meister, Dresden, Germany.*

m.

n.

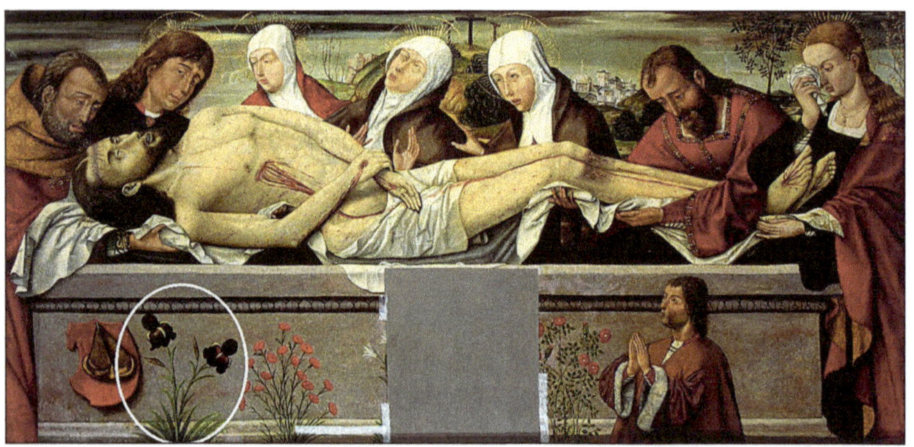

o.

m. Innocenzo da Imola (attr.), Mary Magdalene, 1500, Courtauld Gallery, London, UK.
n. Pietro Perugino, Ascension of Christ, 1510, Cathedral of Sansepolcro, Tuscany, Italy
o. Unknown Spanish artist, The Entombment, 15th century, Hermitage, Saint Petersburg.

**The iris**
The shape of the iris is similar to that of the fleur-de-lis. In Christian art, the iris is used as a secret symbol for the pineal gland. Seemingly casual, this flower shines somewhere in the fore- or background, in a decor with Jesus and or other saints, often in a dark blue or purple color, the color of the energy of the sixth chakra (indigo).

On image m. we see Mary Magdala depicted with a dark iris. That we may interpret the presence of this flower as symbols of a kundalini awakening is confirmed by the clothing of Mary that contains all seven chakra colors.

p.

q.

p. Giovanni Martino Spanzotti and Defendente Ferrari, *The Baptism of Christ*, circa 1540,
   La cattedrale di San Giovanni Battista, Turin, Italy.
q. Eugène Delacroix, *Iris and Skull*, 19th century, The Louvre, Paris, France.

r. Stele (engraved sandstone), 7-8th century, found in Armant, Egypt, Metropolitan Museum of Art, New York, USA.

s. Roman Christian mosaic with Chi-Rho, found at Hinton St Mary, England. Present location: British Museum.

t. Relief, 12th century, Santa Maria de Cóll, Catalonia, Spain.

## 5 Chi-Rho

The Christogram "Chi-Rho" is one of the symbols with which Jesus is indicated.

Chi and Rho are the first two letters of the name Christ in Greek: **ΧΡΙΣΤΟΣ**. This symbol already emerged in the first centuries after Christ. When we inspect the earliest depictions that were found, we see that also in this symbol there is hidden esoteric wisdom.

The rho (P) symbolizes the spinal column with on top the pineal gland, comparable with the staff of the caduceus. The chi (X) represents the two energy channels that merge with a spiritual awakening, after which the pineal gland is stimulated to secrete substances that bring about a divine experience and a vitalization of the body. This physical component is a catalyst in the process of spiritual wakening.

Often the Greek letters alpha and omega are added to the Chi-Rho. The alpha and omega refer to Christ, based on what he says in the Book of Revelation: *I am the Alpha and the Omega, the First and the Last, the Beginning and the End* (Revelation 22:13, also see 1:8).

Alpha and omega are respectively the first and the last letter of the Greek alphabet. Esoterically, they symbolize the polarity of creation. Energetically, they represent the two polar energy channels. The Greek alpha and omega symbols are in some images even connected to the chi (X) of the Chi-Rho. This confirms our esoteric interpretation.

Sometimes we can see an S added to the Chi-Rho monogram, which, esoterically spoken, represents a kundalini-serpent (see image t.).

*u. Five examples of an "overlapping" IHS monogram.*

## 6. IHS

Another centuries old monogram with which Jesus is indicated is IHS. The origin and meaning of this monogram are debated. The most common interpretation is that IHS represents the first three letters of the name Jesus in Greek: (**ΙΗΣ**, Iota, Eta, Sigma). This monogram became particularly popular in the late Middle Ages (circa 1000 - 1250 AD) and became the emblem of the Jesuit order.

IHS is sometimes shown with the three letters overlapping (see u.), because of which the deeper meaning of this monogram appears. We then see a stylized image of the kundalini process: the three energy channels that are involved in a kundalini awakening, with a rising kundalini serpent.

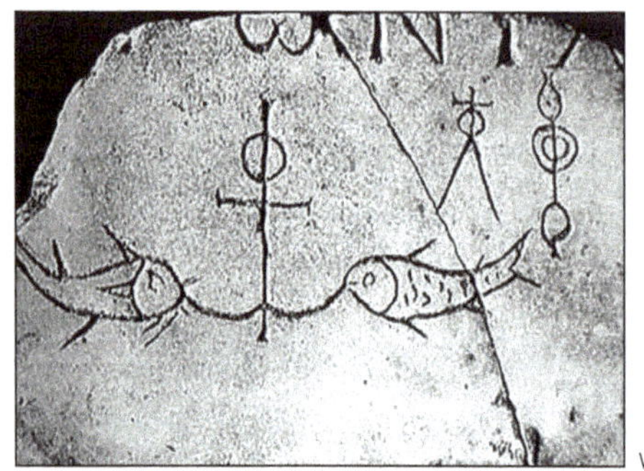

w.

x.

y.

z.

w. From the catacombs of Domitilla, Rome, 3rd century AD.
x. From the catacombs of Prisilla, Rome, 2nd century AD.
y. Tombstone, early 3rd century, the Baths of Diocletian, Rome.
z. Silver ring, 3rd century AD, excavations Roman Fort, Binchester, England.

### 7. The anchor

A symbol that we often see in Christendom is the anchor. The meaning that is commonly given to this symbol is that it represents the aspect "hope" of the three Christian fundaments: faith, hope and love (1 Corinthians 13:13). This meaning is derived from a quote from the apostle Paul from his letter to the Hebrews:

*We have this hope as an anchor for the soul, firm and secure. It enters the inner sanctuary behind the curtain,*
*where Jesus, who went before us, has entered on our behalf. He has become a high priest forever, in the order of Melchizedek.*
(Hebrews 6:19-20)

That the anchor also has an esoteric meaning is confirmed by the addition of two fish, which we see on images from the first two centuries after Christ.
A classical symbol to express the merger of opposites (the sacred marriage) is the *vesica piscis*: a geometric figure of two partly overlapping circles that form two stylized fish.

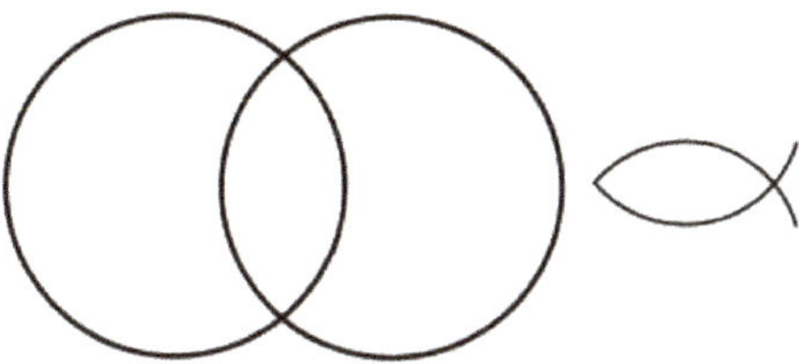

The vesica piscis

The early Christian images unmistakably reflect kundalini symbolism: the anchor represents the spinal column through which the kundalini energy begins to flow when the opposites (the two fish) have merged into oneness. The circle atop the anchor represents the pineal gland, just like with the caduceus.

*On this object from the first centuries after Christ we see a combination of the anchor and the Chi-Rho monogram.*

*From the Godescalc Evangelistary, 781, Bibliothèque nationale de France, Paris.*
*Jesus makes the sign of the sacred marriage.*
*Next to him we see the monograms IHS and Chi-Rho (with an added S).*

# Appendix 2 - More paintings with hidden messages

*Marcantonio Franceschini, Noli Me Tangere ("Don't touch me"), circa 1700, Museum of Fine Arts, Houston.*

With both her left and her right hand, Mary Magdalene makes the sign of the sacred marriage (two fingers together).
The angel in the background does the same with his right hand.

*Hendrick Goltzius, Christ on the Cross, 1600, Staatliche Kunsthalle Karlsruhe, Germany.*

Jesus, his mother Mary and Mary Magdalene make with their right hands the sign of the sacred marriage.
The apostle John resembles a woman. His/her folded hands refer to the spinal column.

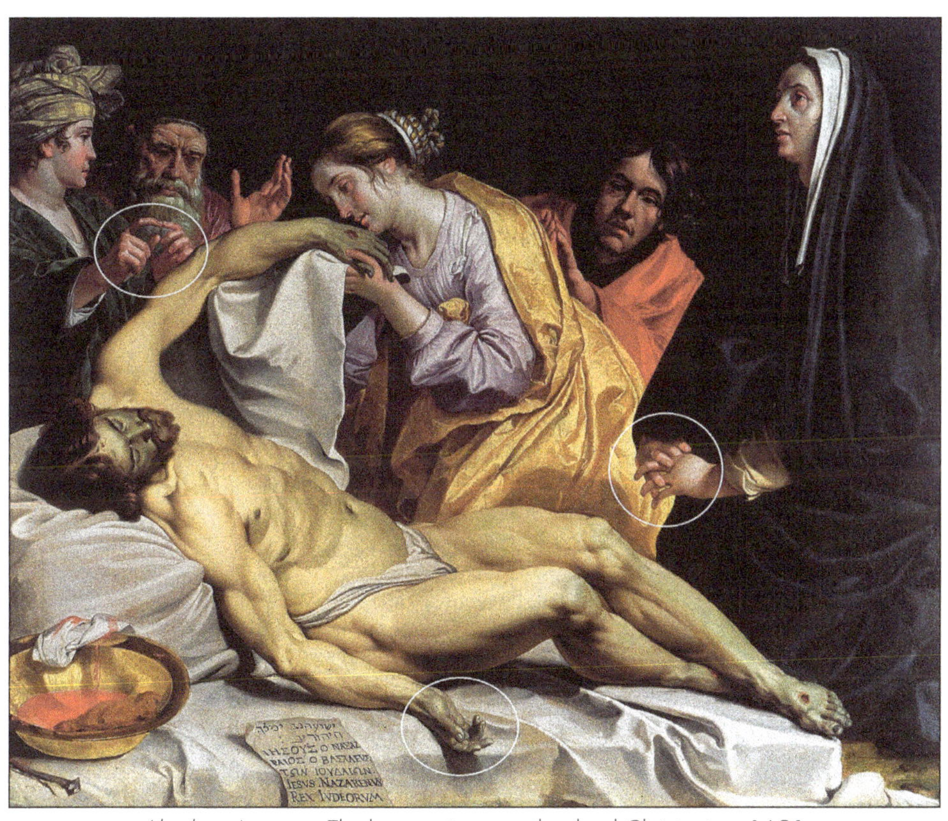



*Abraham Janssens,* The lamentation over the dead Christ, *circa 1621,*
*National Museum in Warshaw, Poland.*

The right hand of Jesus makes the sign of the sacred marriage. The person on the left of the painting makes a gesture that likewise depicts the merger of opposites. The way in which Mary Magdalene hold on to Jesus emphasizes the sacred marriage that transpired internally in Jesus.

The folded hands of Mary, the mother of Jesus, to the right on the painting, refer to the spinal column.

*Maerten de Vos, Christ as a gardener appears to Mary Magdalene, 1646, Rijksmuseum, Amsterdam.*

Both the hands of Jesus and those of Mary Madgalene make the sign of the sacred marriage. Mary uses both her hands. To the left of them are two shrubs that are formed like a pineal gland. The relative position of the shrubs relates to that of Mary and Jesus.

*Maerten de Vos*, triptych with crucifixion, birth and resurrection of Christ, *circa 1570, Kunstpalast, Düsseldorf, Germany.*

Jesus makes the sign of the sacred marriage, both in the crucifixion scene and the resurrection (right panel).

Mary Magdalene, under the cross, points at her head: here everything takes place.

Also Mary, the mother of Jesus, reclining in the foreground, makes the sign of the sacred marriage. Her hand is on the arm of a woman wearing a shawl that is attached to the top of her head: a depiction of the kundalini energy.

*Mariotto di Nardo, The Crucifixion, circa 1385-1405,*
*Pharmacy of Santa Maria Novella, Florence, Italy.*

Mary Magdalene (under the cross) raises two fingers: the sign of the sacred marriage that has taken place within Jesus.
Directly behind her, parallel to her spinal column, is the reed with sponge which is raised to the head of Jesus: a depiction of the kundalini process.

*Parmigianino, Bardi Altarpiece, 1521, church of Santa Maria at Bardi, Italy.*

The evangelist John (second from the left), resembles a woman. He/she holds a cup (a permanent attribute of John) with three serpents. These refer to the three energy channels which are involved with a kundalini awakening.

*Raffaellino del Garbo, Madonna, santi e donatori,*
*Museo del Cenacolo di Andrea del Sarto, Florence, Italy*

The evangelist John (to the right), hides his face behind his hand. The deeper meaning of this is that Mary Magdalene hides her face and pretends to be John in her gospel. Two fingers of this hand (making the sign of the sacred marriage) point at his/her forehead; the place where the inner crucifixion takes place.

*Tintoretto*, The Crucifixion, *16ᵗʰ century, Civic Museums of Padua, Italy.*

Both hands of Jesus make the sign of the sacred marriage. On the back of Mary Magdalene are two strands of hair. These depict the two energy channels that flow left and right of the spinal column and merge in the head: the energetic aspect of the sacred marriage. On the garment of the man to the right of the cross we see ornamentation that refers to the caduceus; the classical symbol for a kundalini awakening. This man hold two cords of his robe in one hand: the merger of the polar energy channels.

*Unknown Artist, Station of the Cross, circa 1900.*

On the sleeve of Mary Magdalene we see an ornamentation shaped like a pineal gland. Her hand is positioned against her head: here the crucifixion takes place…

*Unknown Artist, triptych, 12th century, Ursuline Monastery, Erfurt, Germany.*

The evangelist John (second from the right) resembles a woman and makes the sign of the sacred marriage.

*Georges de La Tour, The Repentant Magdalen, circa 1640,
National Gallery of Art, Washington, USA.*

The burning candle is placed behind the skull, at the center. The tip of the flame peaks over the top of it: a reference to the kundalini fire that flows toward the crown (also think of the Pentecost fire that "descended" upon the apostles). Mary Magdalene points with two fingers (the sign of the sacred marriage) to the forehead of the skull, the place where the crucifixion and the sacred marriage take place.

*Adam Elsheimer, the Altarpiece of the Exaltation of the True Cross, 1605,
the Städel Museum, Frankfurt, Germany.*

Depicted here is the glorification of the cross by the saints, the prophets and the angels. In the foreground, St. Sebastian and the four church fathers Pope Gregory, St. Jerome, St. Ambrose, and St. Augustine discuss with the first Christan martyrs: St. Stephen and St. Laurence.
This picture is centered on Mary Magdalene. Both her hand and the hand of St. Catherine on her shoulder make the sign of the sacred marriage. Three characters in the painting point at Mary Magdalene. With this the artist wants to shed light on both Mary's spiritual status and her significance to the early church.

*Raphael, The Ecstasy of St. Cecilia, 1516-1517,*
*National Art Gallery of Bologna, Italy.*

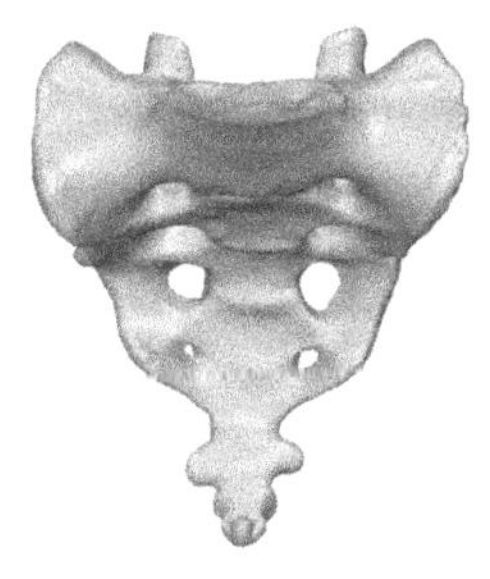

On this painting (left) are depicted from left to right: the apostle Paul, the evangelist John, Saint Cecilia, church father Augustine and Mary Magdalene. On the floor lie the musical instruments of Saint Cecilia, among which a triangle. This refers to the sacrum, which also has the shape of a triangle. The sword of Paul, whose point is placed within the triangle, together with his arm that rests on the sword, depict the kundalini that flows from the sacrum to the head.

To the right on the painting is Mary Magdalene. Her right hand rests on her jar of oil (her attribute). Barely visible, she touches with her middle finger the staff of Saint Augustine. The staff and the middle finger refer to the spinal column through which the divine energy flows. The jar of oil and the staff which Rafael connects this way, are a reference to the spiritual awakening that Mary Magdalene experienced.

Next to Paul stands the apostle John. He looks like a woman (Mary Magdalene is in fact depicted twice on this painting) and makes the sign of the sacred marriage. His/her fingers also touch the sleeve of the arm with which Paul depicts a kundalini awakening: a second reference to the spiritual status of Mary Magdalene.

John/Mary exchange glances with Saint Augustine, who is regarded as one of the most important founders of the Christian church. With this Raphael wants to let us know that Mary too should be regarded as a founder of the church.

The painting is one big tribute to "the disciple whom Jesus loved"!

On the right panel we see Mary Magdalene (to the right, with oil jar), with on the fabric of her upper- and undergarments a pineal gland pattern. With this the artist wants to tell us that Mary's anointing of Jesus represents the activation of the pineal gland.

The flower vase, in the foreground of the left panel, also has a pineal gland pattern. The flowers in this vase include a dark blue iris; the flower that in Renaissance paintings was used as secret symbol for the pineal gland and thus a kundalini awakening (see page 187). Mary, the mother of Jesus, wears a dress with the same dark blue color as the iris: indigo, the color of the sixth chakra. With her hands she forms a triangle; a reference to the sacrum.

*Workshop of the Master of 1518, The Magdalen, 16th century,
National Gallery, London, UK.*

The two braids of Mary Magdalene merge at the level of the oil jar which she holds in her hand. This refers to the two energy channels that merge in the head, after which a process of inner anointing takes place (the change in brain fluid). On Mary's head covering we see a reference to the pineal gland, the tiny organ in our head which plays a central role in the process of inner anointing.

The faces of Jesus and Mary Magdalene are placed next to each other so that they seem one: a reference to the sacred marriage. Jesus is depicted without beard, which is unusual in iconography. This is a reference to the state of androgyny, which is the result of the inner merger of the masculine and feminine.

*Caravaggio, Penitent Magdalene, 1596,*
*Doria Pamphilj Gallery, Rome, Italy.*

On the undergarment of Mary Magdalene is depicted a bowl: a reference to the
Holy Grail. Mary's arms are folded in such a way that the bowl would fit in.
The message is that this legendary Holy Grail (drinking from this Holy Grail
was thought to make immortal) exists within the pelvis of a person, and is a
metaphor for a kundalini awakening. The transparent oil jar next to May has
the form of the pineal gland.

*Workshop of the Master of the Magdalen Legend*, The Magdalene, *circa 1510*,
*National Gallery, London, UK.*

With both hands, Mary Magdalene makes the sign of the sacred marriage. Her
red hair is bound in a long ponytail. This symbolizes the kundalini fire that
flows to the crown, where the inner anointing takes place.

*Rogier van der Weyden,* The Descent from the Cross, *circa 1435,
Prado Museum, Madrid, Spain.*

Mary Magdalene wears a belt with on it the text: IHESVSMARIA (Jesus Mary).
On her right hand she wears a (wedding) ring. Both are references to the inner
sacred marriage which took place in Jesus (and not to a marriage between Mary
and Jesus).

This we can deduce from the other symbolism. With her hands, Mary depicts
a merger of left and right (that is: the polar energy channels left and right of
the spinal column). Between her arms, her headscarf hangs down to her pelvis.
The headscarf depicts the kundalini energy that flows from the pelvis to the
head. The man next to Mary wears a robe with a pattern that refers to the pineal
gland.

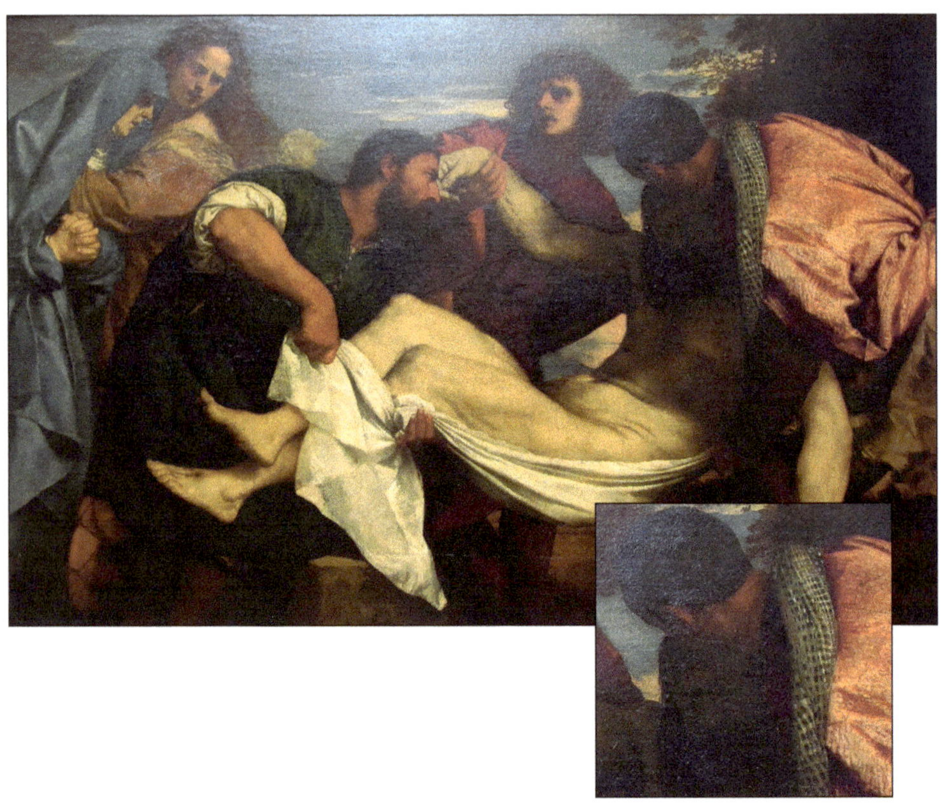



The man to the right on the painting wears a scarf with a "snakeskin print"; a reference to the kundalini serpent.

Mary Magdalene, under the cross, wears a headdress with two long ribbons attached to it. These ribbons symbolize the two energy channels that are involved with a kundalini awakening. The front end of the headdress has the shape of a pine cone and refers to the pineal gland. The physical posture of Mary Magdalene evokes associations with a spiraling (kundalini) serpent.

*Carlo Marochetti, Mary Magdalen Exalted by Angels, Church of Madeleine, Paris, France.*

With this sculpture, the artist proclaims that we should regard the ascension of Mary Magdalene as a metaphor for her kundalini awakening. Mary stands on what seems to be a snakeskin carpet. The circling angels depict the divine energy that moves upward in a spiral motion, from the pelvis to the crown. The intertwined ends of the rope around Mary's waste is a reference to the caduceus. (Also see the next painting.)

218

*Daniele da Volterra, Assumption of the Virgin, early 16 century,
The church of the Santissima Trinità dei Monti, Rome, Italy.*

Mary, the mother of Jesus, ascends into heaven. As with the previous painting, the angels that circle around her depict the spiraling kundalini energy. On the foreground we see a man pointing toward his head with his middle finger: the ascension (that is: the unification with God) is a process that takes place in the head of a person. The middle finger refers to the spinal column with in it the awakened kundalini.

*Andrea di Bartolo, The Last Supper, circa 1420, Pinacoteca Nazionale, Bologna, Italy.*

The apostle reclining against Jesus' bosom looks like a woman. The apostle at the left hand of Jesus raises two fingers: the sign of the sacred marriage.

Jesus points with two fingers to the apostle who is reclining against his bosom:
the sign of the sacred marriage. This apostle points to the fish on the table and
thus refers to the vesica piscis, a symbol that expresses the sacred marriage.

*Dirck Hendricksz, Last Supper, circa 1885, Farnese Gallery, Capodimonte National Museum, Naples, Italy.*

The apostle reclining against Jesus' bosom resembles a woman. Jesus points with his middle finger (symbol of the kundalini energy in the spinal column) at her forehead: here everything takes place…

The apostle who reclines against Jesus' bosom looks like a woman.
The two ribbons that are tied together on the back of the apostle, in the foreground on the right, refer to the two energy channels that merge during a
spiritual awakening at the level of the pineal gland (the knot): the energetic aspect of the sacred marriage that Jesus and Mary Magdalene - in the background
- depict physically.

223

The apostle who leans upon the table in front of Jesus resembles a woman. He/ she makes with the left hand (middle fingers) the sign of the sacred marriage, and so doing points at his/her head. In the foreground we see an apostle who makes the same sign with his hand. The message of the artist is that Jesus and Mary Magdalene together depict the sacred marriage.

*Andrea del Castagno,* Last Supper, *1445-1450,*
*Museo di Cenacolo di Sant'Apollonia, Florence, Italy.*

Jesus makes the sign of the sacred marriage while looking at the disciple who reclines toward him.

The marble panel directly above Jesus shows a remarkable pattern, which differs from the other marble panels, and which strongly resembles a vulva. With this the artist wants to tell us that the apostle next to Jesus is not a man but a woman: Mary Magdalene.

*Last Supper, from the illuminated Ottheinrich Bible, circa 1430.*

The apostle reclining upon Jesus resembles a woman. Jesus makes the sign of the sacred marriage. Barely visible in the aureole of Jesus is a big fleur-de-lis; a reference to the pineal gland (see appendix 2).

*Livio Agresti,* Last Supper, *1572-1575, Oratorio del Gonfalone, Rome, Italy.*

The apostle who reclines against Jesus' bosom looks like a woman. Jesus points with his middle finger at her head. The enormous twisted pillars, with climbing vines, behind them, depict the rising kundalini energy. In the background, Jesus washes the feet of Peter. This washing of the feet is a metaphor of the purifying effect of the kundalini/Holy Spirit. Both in the foreground, and in the top of the paining, above Peter, a hand makes the sign of the sacred marriage.

*Luca Giordano, Penitent Mary Magdalen, 1660-1665,
the Prado Museum, Madrid, Spain.*

Mary studies the Bible and points with her middle finger at her forehead: here the crucifixion takes place…!

*Perugino,* Christ Giving the Keys to St. Peter, *1482, Sistine Chapel, Rome, Italy.*

Jesus delivers the keys to the "Kingdom of Heaven" to Peter. This event from the gospels (Matthew 16:19) caused the Catholic Church to reckon Peter as the first pope. Artist Perugino wants to let us know that this honor is actually Mary Magdalene's. She stands behind Peter in an open posture, because of which she becomes the central figure of the right side of the scene. She is the only one of the apostles who looks at Jesus. The apostle to her left points at her. That this is Mary Magdalene we may deduce from her footwear. All apostles are barefooted. Only Jesus and she wear sandals. Hers are ornamented in such a way that it is clear that this character must be a woman. She holds a small paper scroll in her hand: the gospel she has written!

In the two enormous keys that Peter receives is also a hidden meaning. The vertically hanging lower key - a central element of the painting - symbolizes the spinal column with atop the pineal gland: the "key" to the Kingdom of God is a kundalini awakening!

Also by this author:

# Kundalini Awakening in the Bible
## Many stories, one truth

Within all of us exists the potential for growth that enables us to make the next step in our evolution. This power source is of divine origin and spiritual traditions shared the knowledge of it only with a small group of initiated. The Yoga tradition knows this power source by the name kundalini shakti.

This book introduces the reader to the universal kundalini symbolism that appears in all world religions, and discusses the mysterious source of energy that also provides the central theme of both the Old and the New Testaments.

With many examples, Anne-Marie demonstrates that the entire Bible - from Adam and Eve up to the Book of Revelation - is essentially about a kundalini awakening.

She also shares a remarkable discovery with the reader: the gospel of John, the most mystical of the four gospels in the New Testament, is based on a spiritual journey through the seven chakras. The seven miracles, which Jesus performs, describe the specific effect of a kundalini awakening upon the first to the seventh chakra. This is an entirely new exegetical perspective. As far as is known, nothing has been previously published about this.

According to Jesus, the Pharisees had taken the "key of knowledge" away from believers. With *Kundalini awakening* it is returned to them.

*"Woe to you experts in the law, because you have taken away the key to knowledge. You yourselves have not entered, and you have hindered those who were entering"* (Luke 11:52).

For more information and 16 sample pages, see www.anne-marie.eu/en/

# John the Baptist who became Jesus the Christ

For two thousand years, John the Baptist has been seen as the one who first predicted the coming of the Messiah and subsequently recognized Jesus as "the Lamb of God" at his baptism in the Jordan River.

John the Baptist, however, was not merely the herald of Jesus. He was Jesus. He became a Christos, an anointed one, after his process of God-realization, symbolized by his baptism in the Jordan.

He became the Messiah for whom for centuries the Jews had been eagerly waiting. This Redeemer, however, had to answer to a great number of prophesies from the sacred Jewish Scriptures, and John the Baptist did not do so. And so the evangelists gave him, posthumously, a new name and a new identity, which refers to a character from the Old Testament: Joshua son of Nun, which, freely translated means the son of God.

This book shows how this explosive fact is cryptically woven into the gospel stories: for those who "have ears and want to hear." And while unraveling this great secret, several other inexplicable Biblical puzzle pieces fall into place. The reader obtains insight in what the mysterious Manna was that God made to come down from heaven to feed the people of Israel during their forty year stay in the desert. The rather unbelievable story of Jonah who stayed in the belly of the great fish and emerged alive, is clarified. And additionally, it will be clear why the disciples of Jesus had to cast their nets to the right side of the boat. And much more!

Throughout the centuries there has always been a small group of initiated who knew that John the Baptist was Jesus. This book contains many paintings from old masters like Da Vinci, Michelangelo, Raphael and Correggio, in which this fact is cryptically incorporated. See and judge for yourself!

ISBN:
E-book: 978-90-825023-2-9
Paperback: 978-90-825023-1-2

For more information and a preview of the first 17 pages,
see www.anne-marie.eu/en/

## Colophon

Mary Magdalene, the disciple whom Jesus loved© was written by Anne-Marie Wegh.
www.anne-marie.eu/en/

The cover and layout of this book were designed by Marc Boom.
ISB-nummer 978-90-825023-4-3
NUR: 708

Cover image: Detail of painting Disputation of the Holy Sacrament, by Raffaello Sanzio da Urbino (Raphael), 1510, Apostolic Palace, Vatican City, Rome. See also page 46.

The English edition of this book was produced in the spring of 2022.

Mary Magdalene, the disciple whom Jesus loved© was published by Magdalena Publishers.



Magdalena Publishers
Kerkpad 4a
6631 AB Horssen
The Netherlands
Telephone 0031 6-54 68 34 27

WWW.ANNE-MARIE.EU

www.ingramcontent.com/pod-product-compliance
Lightning Source LLC
LaVergne TN
LVHW051108180726
843512LV00011B/761